We Go Through to Get To

(Our God Given Purpose)

Barbara J. Tolbert

authorHOUSE®

AuthorHouse™
1663 Liberty Drive
Bloomington, IN 47403
www.authorhouse.com
Phone: 1 (800) 839-8640

Published by AuthorHouse 05/06/2019

ISBN: 978-1-5462-7952-5 (sc)
ISBN: 978-1-5462-7950-1 (hc)
ISBN: 978-1-5462-7951-8 (e)

Library of Congress Control Number: 2019901388

Print information available on the last page.

Contents

According to Scripture we all have a purpose for being alive. We may not all look, talk, walk or speak in the same manner but that does not mean we are any less valuable. "Jeremiah 1:5 reads, Before I formed thee in the belly I knew thee; and before thou camest forth out of the womb I sanctified thee, and I ordained thee a prophet unto the nations." "Jeremiah 29:11 reads, For I know the thoughts that I think toward you, saith the LORD, thoughts of peace, and not of evil, to give you an expected end." We have to go through some things, pain, hardship, sorrow disappointment, discouragement and disrespect to get to the position GOD has for us.

When you look back at some of the places we have been, people we have connected with, jobs we have worked, and wondered why or how we ended up doing what we did, remember it was by design. We were set up for the position we were destined to work in for the glory of GOD. People in this book were not perfect, and I have news for you, neither are we. These people went through some things, either by choice or not, and eventually ended where they were supposed to be in the LORD. My call to you is do not give up. No matter what the circumstance, no matter how much pain, even if you do not understand, remember this GOD has a plan for your life!

A Certain Man Was Blind From Birth

Christ cured many who were blind by disease or accident; here he cured one born blind. Thus he showed his power to help in the most desperate cases, and the work of his grace upon the souls of sinners, which gives sight to those blind by nature. This poor man could not see Christ, but Christ saw him. And if we know or apprehend anything of Christ, it is because we were first known of him. Christ says of uncommon calamities, that they are not always to be looked on as special punishments of sin; sometimes they are for the glory of God, and to manifest his works. Our life is our day, in which it concerns us to do the work of the day. We must be busy, and not waste day-time; it will be time to rest when our day is done, for it is but a day. The approach of death should quicken us to improve all our opportunities of doing and getting good. What good we have an opportunity to do, we should do quickly. And he that will never do a good work till there is nothing to be objected against, will leave many a good work for ever undone' Christ magnified his power, in making a blind man to see, doing that which one would think more likely to make a seeing man blind. Human reason cannot judge of the Lord's methods; he uses means and instruments that men despise. Those that would be healed by Christ must be ruled by him. He came back from the pool wondering and wondered at; he came seeing. This represents the benefits in attending on ordinances of Christ's appointment; souls go weak, and come away strengthened; go doubting, and come away satisfied; go mourning, and come away rejoicing; go blind, and come away seeing.

John 9:1-12

And as *Jesus* passed by, he saw a man which was blind from *his* birth.

And his disciples asked him, saying, Master, who did sin, this man, or his parents, that he was born blind?

Jesus answered, Neither hath this man sinned, nor his parents: but that the works of God should be made manifest in him.

I must work the works of him that sent me, while it is day: the night cometh, when no man can work.

As long as I am in the world, I am the light of the world.

When he had thus spoken, he spat on the ground, and made clay of the spittle, and he anointed the eyes of the blind man with the clay,

And said unto him, Go, wash in the pool of Siloam, (which is by interpretation, Sent.) He went his way therefore, and washed, and came seeing.

The neighbors therefore, and they which before had seen him that he was blind, said, Is not this he that sat and begged?

Some said, This is he: others *said*, He is like him: *but* he said, I am *he*.

Therefore said they unto him, How were thine eyes opened?

He answered and said, A man that is called Jesus made clay, and anointed mine eyes, and said unto me, Go to the pool of Siloam, and wash: and I went and washed, and I received sight.

Then said they unto him, Where is he? He said, I know not.

A Certain Widow's Only Son Died

When the Lord saw the poor widow following her son to the grave, he had compassion on her. See Christ's power over death itself. The gospel calls to all people, to young people particularly, is, Arise from the dead, and Christ shall give you light and life. When Christ put life into him, it appeared by the youth's sitting up. Have we grace from Christ? Let us show it. He began to speak: whenever Christ gives us spiritual life, he opens the lips in prayer and praise. When dead souls are raised to spiritual life, by Divine power going with the gospel, we must glorify God, and look upon it as a gracious visit to his people. Let us seek for such an interest in our compassionate Saviour, that we may look forward with joy to the time when the Redeemer's voice shall call forth all that are in their graves. May we be called to the resurrection of life, not to that of damnation.

Luke 7:11-17

And it came to pass the day after, that he went into a city called Nain; and many of his disciples went with him, and much people.

12 Now when he came nigh to the gate of the city, behold, there was a dead man carried out, the only son of his mother, and she was a widow: and much people of the city was with her.

13 And when the Lord saw her, he had compassion on her, and said unto her, Weep not.

14 And he came and touched the bier: and they that bare *him* stood still. And he said, Young man, I say unto thee, Arise.

15 And he that was dead sat up, and began to speak. And he delivered him to his mother.

16 And there came a fear on all: and they glorified God, saying, That a
great prophet is risen up among us; and, That God hath visited his people.
17 And this rumour of him went forth throughout all Judaea, and
throughout all the region round about.

A Certain Woman Had An Issue Of Blood For 12 Years

A despised gospel will go where it will be better received. One of the rulers of a synagogue earnestly besought Christ for a little daughter, about twelve years old, who was dying. Another cure was wrought by the way. We should do good, not only when in the house, but when we walk by the way, It is common with people not to apply to Christ till they have tried in vain all other helpers, and find them, as certainly they will, physicians of no value. Some run to diversions and gay company; others plunge into business, or even into intemperance; others go about to establish their own righteousness, or torment themselves by vain superstitions. Many perish in these ways; but none will ever find rest to the soul by such devices; while those whom Christ heals of the disease of sin, find in themselves an entire change for the better. As secret acts of sin, so secret acts of faith, are known to the Lord Jesus. The woman told all the truth. It is the will of Christ that his people should be comforted, and he has power to command comfort to troubled spirits. The more simply we depend on Him, and expect great things from him, the more we shall find in ourselves that he is become our salvation. Those who, by faith, are healed of their spiritual diseases, have reason to go in peace.

Mark 5:25-34; Matthew 9:22; Luke 8:43-48

25 And a certain woman, which had an issue of blood twelve years,

26 And had suffered many things of many physicians, and had spent all that she had, and was nothing bettered, but rather grew worse,

27 When she had heard of Jesus, came in the press behind, and touched his garment.

28 For she said, If I may touch but his clothes, I shall be whole.

29 And straightway the fountain of her blood was dried up; and she felt in *her* body that she was healed of that plague.

30 And Jesus, immediately knowing in himself that virtue had gone out of him, turned him about in the press, and said, Who touched my clothes?

31 And his disciples said unto him, Thou seest the multitude thronging thee, and sayest thou, Who touched me?

32 And he looked round about to see her that had done this thing.

33 But the woman fearing and trembling, knowing what was done in her, came and fell down before him, and told him all the truth.

34 And he said unto her, Daughter, thy faith hath made thee whole; go in peace, and be whole of thy plague.

A Certain Woman Ran Out Of Meal

God wonderfully suits men to the work he designs them for. The times were fit for an Elijah; an Elijah was fit for them. The Spirit of the Lord knows how to fit men for the occasions. Elijah let Ahab know that God was displeased with the idolaters, and would chastise them by the want of rain, which it was not in the power of the gods they served to bestow. Elijah was commanded to hide himself. If Providence calls us to solitude and retirement, it becomes us to go: when we cannot be useful, we must be patient; and when we cannot work for God, we must sit still quietly for him. The ravens were appointed to bring him meat, and did so. Let those who have but from hand to mouth, learn to live upon Providence, and trust it for the bread of the day, in the day. God could have sent angels to minister to him; but he chose to show that he can serve his own purposes by the meanest creatures, as effectually as by the mightiest. Elijah seems to have continued thus above a year. The natural supply of water, which came by common providence, failed; but the miraculous supply of food, made sure to him by promise, failed not. If the heavens fail, the earth fails of course; such are all our creature-comforts: we lose them when we most need them, like brooks in summer. But there is a river which makes glad the city of God, that never runs dry, a well of water that springs up to eternal life. Lord, give us that living water! Many widows were in Israel in the days of Elias, and some, it is likely, would have bidden him welcome to their houses; yet he is sent to honor and bless with his presence a city of Sidon, a Gentile city, and so becomes the first prophet of the Gentiles. Jezebel was Elijah's greatest enemy; yet, to show her how powerless was her malice, God will find a hiding-place for him even in her own country. The person appointed to entertain Elijah is not one of the rich or great men of Sidon; but a poor widow woman, in want, and desolate, is made both able and willing to sustain him. It is God's way, and it is his glory, to make use of, and put honor upon, the weak and foolish things of the world. O woman, great was thy faith; one has not found the like, no not in Israel. She took the prophet's word, that she should not lose by it. Those who can venture upon the promise of God, will make no difficulty to expose and empty themselves in his service, by giving him his part first. Surely the increase of this widow's faith, so as to enable her thus readily to deny herself, and to depend upon the Divine promise, was as great a miracle in the kingdom of grace, as the increase of her meal and oil in the kingdom of providence. Happy are all who can thus, against hope, believe and obey in hope. One poor meal's meat this poor widow gave the prophet; in recompense of it, she and her son did eat above two years, in a time of famine. To have food from God's special favor, and in such good company as Elijah, made it more than doubly sweet. It is promised to those who trust in God, that they shall not be ashamed in evil time; in days of famine they shall be satisfied.

1 Kings 17:8-16

8 And the word of the LORD came unto him, saying,

9 Arise, get thee to Zarephath, which *belongeth* to Zidon, and dwell there: behold, I have commanded a widow woman there to sustain thee.

10 So he arose and went to Zarephath. And when he came to the gate of the city, behold, the widow woman *was* there gathering of sticks: and he called to her, and said, Fetch me, I pray thee, a little water in a vessel, that I may drink.

11 And as she was going to fetch *it*, he called to her, and said, Bring me, I pray thee, a morsel of bread in thine hand.

12 And she said, *As* the LORD thy God liveth, I have not a cake, but an handful of meal in a barrel, and a little oil in a cruse: and, behold, I *am* gathering two sticks, that I may go in and dress it for me and my son, that we may eat it, and die.

13 And Elijah said unto her, Fear not; go *and* do as thou hast said: but make me thereof a little cake first, and bring *it* unto me, and after make for thee and for thy son.

14 For thus saith the LORD God of Israel, The barrel of meal shall not waste, neither shall the cruse of oil fail, until the day *that* the LORD sendeth rain upon the earth.

15 And she went and did according to the saying of Elijah: and she, and he, and her house, did eat *many* days.

16 *And* the barrel of meal wasted not, neither did the cruse of oil fail, according to the word of the LORD, which he spake by Elijah.

A Certain Woman Was Threatened That Her Children Had To Go To A Debtor's Prison

Elisha's miracles were acts of real charity: Christ's were so; not only great wonders, but great favors to those for whom they were wrought. God magnifies his goodness with his power. Elisha readily received a poor widow's complaint. Those that leave their families under a load of debt, know not what trouble they cause. It is the duty of all who profess to follow the Lord, while they trust to God for daily bread, not to tempt him by carelessness or extravagance, nor to contract debts; for nothing tends more to bring reproach upon the gospel, or distresses their families more when they are gone. Elisha put the widow in a way to pay her debt, and to maintain herself and her family. This was done by miracle, but so as to show what is the best method to assist those who are in distress, which is, to help them to improve by their own industry what little they have. The oil, sent by miracle, continued flowing as long as she had empty vessels to receive it. We are never straitened in God, or in the riches of his grace; all our straightness is in ourselves. It is our faith that fails, not his promise. He gives more than we ask: were there more vessels, there is enough in God to fill them; enough for all, enough for each; and the Redeemer's all-sufficiency will only be stayed from the supplying the wants of sinners and saving their souls, when no more apply to him for salvation. The widow must pay her debt with the money she received for her oil. Though her creditors were too hard with her, yet they must be paid, even before she made any provision for her children. It is one of the main laws of the Christian religion, that we pay every just debt, and give everyone his own, though we leave ever so little for ourselves; and this, not of constraint, but for conscience' sake. Those who bear an honest mind, cannot with pleasure eat their daily bread, unless it be their own bread. She and her children must live upon the rest; that is, upon the money received for the oil, with which they must put themselves into a way to get an honest livelihood. We cannot now expect miracles, yet we may expect mercies, if we wait on God, and seek to him. Let widows in particular depend upon him. He that has all hearts in his hand, can, without a miracle, send as effectual a supply.

2 Kings 4:1-7

Now there cried a certain woman of the wives of the sons of the
prophets unto Elisha, saying, Thy servant my husband is dead; and thou
knowest that thy servant did fear the LORD: and the creditor is come to
take unto him my two sons to be bondmen.
2 And Elisha said unto her, What shall I do for thee? tell me, what
hast thou in the house? And she said, Thine handmaid hath not any thing
in the house, save a pot of oil.
3 Then he said, Go, borrow thee vessels abroad of all thy neighbours,
even empty vessels; borrow not a few.
4 And when thou art come in, thou shalt shut the door upon thee and
upon thy sons, and shalt pour out into all those vessels, and thou shalt set
aside that which is full.
5 So she went from him, and shut the door upon her and upon her
sons, who brought *the vessels* to her; and she poured out.
6 And it came to pass, when the vessels were full, that she said unto
her son, Bring me yet a vessel. And he said unto her, *There is* not a vessel
more. And the oil stayed.
7 Then she came and told the man of God. And he said, Go, sell the
oil, and pay thy debt, and live thou and thy children of the rest.

Ahab Was Henpecked

When, instead of a help meet, a man has an agent for Satan, in the form of an artful, unprincipled, yet beloved wife, fatal effects may be expected. Never were more wicked orders given by any prince, than those Jezebel sent to the rulers of Jezreel. Naboth must be murdered under color of religion. There is no wickedness so vile, so horrid, but religion has sometimes been made a cover for it. Also, it must be done under color of justice, and with the formalities of legal process. Let us, from this sad story, be amazed at the wickedness of the wicked, and the power of Satan in the children of disobedience. Let us commit the keeping of our lives and comforts to God, for innocence will not always be our security; and let us rejoice in the knowledge that all will be set to rights in the great day.

But there was none like unto Ahab, which did sell himself to work wickedness in the sight of the LORD, whom Jezebel his wife stirred up.

1 Kings 21:1-7

And it came to pass after these things, *that* Naboth the Jezreelite had a vineyard, which *was* in Jezreel, hard by the palace of Ahab king of Samaria.
2 And Ahab spake unto Naboth, saying, Give me thy vineyard, that I may have it for a garden of herbs, because it *is* near unto my house: and I will give thee for it a better vineyard than it; *or*, if it seem good to thee, I will give thee the worth of it in money.
3 And Naboth said to Ahab, The LORD forbid it me, that I should give the inheritance of my fathers unto thee.
4 And Ahab came into his house heavy and displeased because of the word which Naboth the Jezreelite had spoken to him: for he had said, I will

not give thee the inheritance of my fathers. And he laid him down upon
his bed, and turned away his face, and would eat no bread.

5 But Jezebel his wife came to him, and said unto him, Why is thy
spirit so sad, that thou eatest no bread?

6 And he said unto her, Because I spake unto Naboth the Jezreelite,
and said unto him, Give me thy vineyard for money; or else, if it please
thee, I will give thee *another* vineyard for it: and he answered, I will not
give thee my vineyard.

7 And Jezebel his wife said unto him, Dost thou now govern the
kingdom of Israel? arise, *and* eat bread, and let thine heart be merry: I will
give thee the vineyard of Naboth the Jezreelite.

Barak Was So Afraid That A Woman Had To Fight His Battle

Deborah was a prophetess; one instructed in Divine knowledge by the inspiration of the Spirit of God. She judged Israel as God's mouth to them; correcting abuses, and redressing grievances. By God's direction, she ordered Barak to raise an army, and engage Jabin's forces. Barak insisted much upon her presence. Deborah promised to go with him. She would not send him where she would not go herself. Those who in God's name call others to their duty, should be ready to assist them in it. Barak values the satisfaction of his mind, and the good success of his enterprise, more than mere honour.

Judges 4: 4-8

4 And Deborah, a prophetess, the wife of Lapidoth, she judged Israel at that time.

5 And she dwelt under the palm tree of Deborah between Ramah and Bethel in mount Ephraim: and the children of Israel came up to her for judgment.

6 And she sent and called Barak the son of Abinoam out of Kedeshnaphtali, and said unto him, Hath not the LORD God of Israel commanded, *saying*, Go and draw toward mount Tabor, and take with thee ten thousand men of the children of Naphtali and of the children of Zebulun?

7 And I will draw unto thee to the river Kishon Sisera, the captain of Jabin's army, with his chariots and his multitude; and I will deliver him into thine hand.

8 And Barak said unto her, If thou wilt go with me, then I will go: but if thou wilt not go with me, *then* I will not go.

David Took What Didn't Belong To Him

See how the way of sin is down-hill; when men begin to do evil, they cannot soon stop. Observe the aggravations of the sin. How could David rebuke or punish that in others, of which he was conscious that he himself was guilty?

Giving way to sin hardens the heart, and provokes the departure of the Holy Spirit. Robbing a man of his reason, is worse than robbing him of his money; and drawing him into sin, is worse than drawing him into any worldly trouble whatever.

Adulteries often occasion murders, and one wickedness is sought to be covered by another. The beginnings of sin are much to be dreaded; for who knows where they will end? Can a real believer ever tread this path? Can such a person be indeed a child of God? Though grace be not lost in such an awful case, the assurance and consolation of it must be suspended. All David's life, spirituality, and comfort in religion, we may be sure were lost. No man in such a case can have evidence to be satisfied that he is a believer. The higher a man's confidence is, who has sunk in wickedness, the greater his presumption and hypocrisy. Let not anyone who resembles David in nothing but his transgressions, bolster up his confidence with this example. Let him follow David in his humiliation, repentance, and his other eminent graces, before he thinks himself only a backslider, and not a hypocrite. Let no opposer of the truth say. These are the fruits of faith! No; they are the effects of corrupt nature. Let us all watch against the beginnings of self-indulgence, and keep at the utmost distance from all evil. But with the Lord there is mercy and plenteous redemption. He will cast out no humble, penitent believer; nor will he suffer Satan to pluck his sheep out of his hand. Yet the Lord will recover his people, in such a way as will mark his abhorrence of their crimes, to hinder all who regard his word from abusing the encouragements of his mercy.

2 Samuel 11-1-3, 27

1. And it came to pass, after the year was expired, at the time when kings go forth *to battle*, that David sent Joab, and his servants with him, and all Israel; and they destroyed the children of Ammon, and besieged Rabbah. But David tarried still at Jerusalem.

2 And it came to pass in an eveningtide, that David arose from off his bed, and walked upon the roof of the king's house: and from the roof he saw a woman washing herself; and the woman *was* very beautiful to look upon.

3 And David sent and enquired after the woman. And *one* said, *Is* not this Bathsheba, the daughter of Eliam, the wife of Uriah the Hittite?

27 And when the mourning was past, David sent and fetched her to his house, and she became his wife, and bare him a son. But the thing that David had done displeased the LORD.

Dorcas Died, And Peter Brought Her Back To Life

Many are full of good words, who are empty and barren in good works; but Tabitha was a great doer, no great talker. Christians who have not property to give in charity, may yet be able to do acts of charity, working with their hands, or walking with their feet, for the good of others. Those are certainly best praised whose own works praise them, whether the words of others do so or not. But such are ungrateful indeed, who have kindness shown them, and will not acknowledge it, by showing the kindness that has done them. While we live upon the fulness of Christ for our whole salvation, we should desire to be full of good works, for the honor of his name, and for the benefit of his saints. Such characters as Dorcas are useful where they dwell, as showing the excellency of the word of truth by their lives. How mean then the cares of the numerous females who seek no distinction but outward decoration, and who waste their lives in the trifling pursuits of dress and vanity! Power went along with the word, and Dorcas came to life. Thus, in the raising of dead souls to spiritual life, the first sign of life is the opening of the eyes of the mind. Here we see that the Lord can make up every loss; that he overrules every event for the good of those who trust in him, and for the glory of his name.

Acts 9:36-42

Now there was at Joppa a certain disciple named Tabitha, which by
interpretation is called Dorcas: this woman was full of good works and
almsdeeds which she did.
37 And it came to pass in those days, that she was sick, and died:
whom when they had washed, they laid *her* in an upper chamber.

38 And forasmuch as Lydda was nigh to Joppa, and the disciples had heard that Peter was there, they sent unto him two men, desiring *him* that he would not delay to come to them.

39 Then Peter arose and went with them. When he was come, they brought him into the upper chamber: and all the widows stood by him weeping, and shewing the coats and garments which Dorcas made, while she was with them.

40 But Peter put them all forth, and kneeled down, and prayed; and turning *him* to the body said, Tabitha, arise. And she opened her eyes: and when she saw Peter, she sat up.

41 And he gave her *his* hand, and lifted her up, and when he had called the saints and widows, presented her alive.

42 And it was known throughout all Joppa; and many believed in the Lord.

Eli Was Nearly Blind And When He Heard The News Of The Death Of His Evil Sons He Fell Backward And Broke His Neck

The defeat of the army was very grievous to Eli as a judge; the tidings of the death of his two sons, to whom he had been so indulgent, and who, as he had reason to fear, died impenitent, touched him as a father; yet there was a greater concern on his spirit. And when the messenger concluded his story with, "The ark of God is taken," he is struck to the heart, and died immediately. A man may die miserably, yet not die eternally; may come to an untimely end, yet the end be peace.

1 Samuel 4:15-18

Now Eli was ninety and eight years old; and his eyes were dim, that he could not see.

16 And the man said unto Eli, I *am* he that came out of the army, and I fled to day out of the army. And he said, What is there done, my son?

17 And the messenger answered and said, Israel is fled before the Philistines, and there hath been also a great slaughter among the people, and thy two sons also, Hophni and Phinehas, are dead, and the ark of God is taken.

18 And it came to pass, when he made mention of the ark of God, that he fell from off the seat backward by the side of the gate, and his neck brake, and he died: for he was an old man, and heavy. And he had judged Israel forty years.

Elijah Had A Pity Party

Jezebel sent Elijah a threatening message. Carnal hearts are hardened and enraged against God, by that which should convince and conquer them. Great faith is not always alike strong. He might be serviceable to Israel at this time, and had all reason to depend upon God's protection, while doing God's work; yet he flees. His was not the deliberate desire of grace, as Paul's, to depart and be with Christ. God thus left Elijah to himself, to show that when he was bold and strong, it was in the Lord, and the power of his might; but of himself he was no better than his fathers. God knows what he designs us for, though we do not, what services, what trials, and he will take care that we are furnished with grace sufficient.

1 Kings 19:1-4

And Ahab told Jezebel all that Elijah had done, and withal how he had slain all the prophets with the sword.

2 Then Jezebel sent a messenger unto Elijah, saying, So let the gods do *to me*, and more also, if I make not thy life as the life of one of them by to morrow about this time.

3 And when he saw *that*, he arose, and went for his life, and came to Beersheba, which *belongeth* to Judah, and left his servant there.

4 But he himself went a day's journey into the wilderness, and came and sat down under a juniper tree: and he requested for himself that he might die; and said, It is enough; now, O LORD, take away my life; for I *am* not better than my fathers

Elisha Cursed 42 Children And They Were Killed By A Bear Because They Called Him A Bald Head

Here is a curse on the youths of Bethel, enough to destroy them; it was not a curse causeless, for it was Elisha's character, as God's prophet, that they abused. They bade him "go up," reflecting on the taking up of Elijah into heaven. The prophet acted by Divine impulse. If the Holy Spirit had not directed Elisha's solemn curse, the providence of God would not have followed it with judgment. The Lord must be glorified as a righteous God who hates sin, and will reckon for it. Let young persons be afraid of speaking wicked words, for God notices what they say. Let them not mock at any for defects in mind or body; especially it is at their peril, if they scoff at any for well doing. Let parents that would have comfort in their children, train them up well, and do their utmost betimes to drive out the foolishness that is bound up in their hearts. And what will be the anguish of those parents, at the day of judgment, who witness the everlasting condemnation of their offspring, occasioned by their own bad example, carelessness, or wicked teaching!

2 Kings 2 23-24;

23 And he went up from thence unto Bethel: and as he was going up by the way, there came forth little children out of the city, and mocked him, and said unto him, Go up, thou bald head; go up, thou bald head.

24 And he turned back, and looked on them, and cursed them in the name of the LORD. And there came forth two she bears out of the wood, and tare forty and two children of them.

Esau Thought More Of Food Than His Birthright

We have here the bargain made between Jacob and Esau about the right, which was Esau's by birth, but Jacob's by promise. It was for a spiritual privilege; and we see Jacob's desire of the birth-right, but he sought to obtain it by crooked courses, not like his character as a plain man. He was right, that he coveted earnestly the best gifts; he was wrong, that he took advantage of his brother's need. The inheritance of their father's worldly goods did not descend to Jacob, and was not meant in this proposal. But it included the future possession of the land of Canaan by his children's children, and the covenant made with Abraham as to Christ the promised Seed. Believing Jacob valued these above all things; unbelieving Esau despised them. Yet although we must be of Jacob's judgment in seeking the birth-right, we ought carefully to avoid all guile, in seeking to obtain even the greatest advantages. Jacob's pottage pleased Esau's eye. "Give me some of that red;" for this he was called Edom, or Red. Gratifying the sensual appetite ruins thousands of precious souls. When men's hearts walk after their own eyes, and when they serve their own bellies, they are sure to be punished. If we use ourselves to deny ourselves, we break the force of most temptations. It cannot be supposed that Esau was dying of hunger in Isaac's house. The words signify, I am going towards death; he seems to mean, I shall never live to inherit Canaan, or any of those future supposed blessings; and what signifies it who has them when I am dead and gone. This would be the language of profaneness, with which the apostle brands him and this contempt of the birth-right is blamed. It is the greatest folly to part with our interest in God, and Christ, and heaven, for the riches, honors, and pleasures of this world; it is as bad a bargain as his who sold a birth-right for a dish of pottage. Esau ate and drank, pleased his palate, satisfied his appetite, and then carelessly rose up and went his way, without any serious thought, or any regret, about the bad bargain he had made. Thus, Esau despised his birth-right. By his neglect and contempt afterwards, and by justifying himself in what he had done, he put the bargain past recall. People are ruined, not so much by doing what is amiss, as by doing it and not repenting of it.

Genesis 25:27-34

27 And the boys grew: and Esau was a cunning hunter, a man of the field; and Jacob *was* a plain man, dwelling in tents.

28 And Isaac loved Esau, because he did eat of *his* venison: but Rebekah loved Jacob.

29 And Jacob sod pottage: and Esau came from the field, and he *was* faint:

30 And Esau said to Jacob, Feed me, I pray thee, with that same red *pottage*; for I *am* faint: therefore was his name called Edom.

31 And Jacob said, Sell me this day thy birthright.

32 And Esau said, Behold, I *am* at the point to die: and what profit shall this birthright do to me?

33 And Jacob said, Swear to me this day; and he sware unto him: and he sold his birthright unto Jacob.

34 Then Jacob gave Esau bread and pottage of lentiles; and he did eat and drink, and rose up, and went his way: thus Esau despised *his* birthright.

Ezekiel Had To Sleep On One Side Half A Year And The Other Side The Other Half Of The Year

The siege of Jerusalem. The prophet was to represent the siege of Jerusalem by signs. He was to lie on his left side for a number of days, supposed to be equal to the years from the establishment of idolatry. All that the prophet sets before the children of his people, about the destruction of Jerusalem, is to show that sin is the provoking cause of the ruin of that once flourishing city.

Ezekiel 4:4-8

4 Lie thou also upon thy left side, and lay the iniquity of the house of Israel upon it: *according* to the number of the days that thou shalt lie upon it thou shalt bear their iniquity.

5 For I have laid upon thee the years of their iniquity, according to the number of the days, three hundred and ninety days: so shalt thou bear the iniquity of the house of Israel.

6 And when thou hast accomplished them, lie again on thy right side, and thou shalt bear the iniquity of the house of Judah forty days: I have appointed thee each day for a year.

7 Therefore thou shalt set thy face toward the siege of Jerusalem, and thine arm *shall be* uncovered, and thou shalt prophesy against it.

8 And, behold, I will lay bands upon thee, and thou shalt not turn thee from one side to another, till thou hast ended the days of thy siege.

Ezekiel Was Commanded Not To Mourn His Beloved Wife

Though mourning for the dead is a duty, yet it must be kept under by religion and right reason: we must not sorrow as men that have no hope. Believers must not copy the language and expressions of those who know not God. The people asked the meaning of the sign. God takes from them all that was dearest to them. And as Ezekiel wept not for his affliction, so neither should they weep for theirs. Blessed be God, we need not pine away under our afflictions; for should all comforts fail, and all sorrows be united, yet the broken heart and the mourner's prayer are always acceptable before God.

Ezekiel 24:15-18

15Also the word of the LORD came unto me, saying,

16 Son of man, behold, I take away from thee the desire of thine eyes with a stroke: yet neither shalt thou mourn nor weep, neither shall thy tears run down.

17 Forbear to cry, make no mourning for the dead, bind the tire of thine head upon thee, and put on thy shoes upon thy feet, and cover not *thy* lips, and eat not the bread of men.

18 So I spake unto the people in the morning: and at even my wife died; and I did in the morning as I was commanded.

Ezekiel Was Commanded To Cook His Food Using Human Dung As Fuel

The bread which was Ezekiel's support, was to be made of coarse grain and pulse mixed together, seldom used except in times of urgent scarcity, and of this he was only to take a small quantity. Thus, was figured the extremity to which the Jews were to be reduced during the siege and captivity. Ezekiel does not plead, Lord, from my youth I have been brought up delicately, and never used to anything like this; but that he had been brought up conscientiously, and never had eaten anything forbidden by the law. It will be comfortable when we are brought to suffer hardships, if our hearts can witness that we have always been careful to keep even from the appearance of evil. See what woeful work sin makes, and acknowledge the righteousness of God herein. Their plenty having been abused to luxury and excess, they were justly punished by famine. When men serve not God with cheerfulness in the abundance of all things, God will make them serve their enemies in the want of all things.

Ezekiel 4:9-17

Take thou also unto thee wheat, and barley, and beans, and lentiles, and millet, and fitches, and put them in one vessel, and make thee bread thereof, *according* to the number of the days that thou shalt lie upon thy side, three hundred and ninety days shalt thou eat thereof.

10 And thy meat which thou shalt eat *shall be* by weight, twenty shekels a day: from time to time shalt thou eat it.

11 Thou shalt drink also water by measure, the sixth part of an hin: from time to time shalt thou drink.

12 And thou shalt eat it *as* barley cakes, and thou shalt bake it with dung that cometh out of man, in their sight.

Hagar Was Mistreated By Sarah, And The Father Of Her Child Put Her Out With Barely Enough To Eat Or Drink

Sarai, no longer expecting to have children herself, proposed to Abram to take another wife, whose children she might; her slave, whose children would be her property. This was done without asking counsel of the Lord. Unbelief worked, God's almighty power was forgotten. It was a bad example, and a source of manifold uneasiness. In every relation and situation in life there is some cross for us to bear: much of the exercise of faith consists in patiently submitting, in waiting the Lord's time, and using only those means which he appoints for the removal of the cross. Foul temptations may have very fair pretenses, and be colored with that which is very plausible. Fleshly wisdom puts us out of God's way. This would not be the case, if we would ask counsel of God by his word and by prayer, before we attempt that which is doubtful. Abram's unhappy marriage to Hagar very soon made a great deal of mischief. We may thank ourselves for the guilt and grief that follow us, when we go out of the way of our duty. See it in this case, Passionate people often quarrel with others, for things of which they themselves must bear the blame. Sarai had given her maid to Abram, yet she cries out, My wrong be upon thee. That is never said wisely, which pride, and anger put into our mouths. Those are not always in the right, who are most loud and forward in appealing to God: such rash and bold imprecations commonly speak guilt and a bad cause. Hagar forgot that she herself had first given the provocation, by despising her mistress. Those that suffer for their faults, ought to bear it patiently.

Hagar was out of her place, and out of the way of her duty, and going further astray, when the Angel found her. It is a great mercy to be stopped in a sinful way, either by conscience or by providence. Whence comest thou? Consider that thou art running from duty, and the privileges thou wast blest with in Abram's tent. It is good to live in a religious family, which those ought to consider who have this advantage. Whither wilt thou go? Thou art running into sin; if Hagar return to Egypt, she will return to idol gods, and into danger in the wilderness through which she must travel. Recollecting who we are, would often teach us our duty. Inquiring whence we came, would show us our sin and folly. Considering whither we shall go, discovers our danger and misery. And those who leave their space and duty, must hasten their return, how mortifying it be. The declaration of the Angel, "I will," shows this Angel was the eternal Word and Son of God. Hagar could not but admire the Lord's mercy, and feel, Have I, who am so unworthy, been favored with a gracious visit from the Lord? She was brought to a better temper, returned, and by her behavior softened Sarai, and received more gentle treatment.

Genesis 16:9-14

9 And Sarah saw the son of Hagar the Egyptian, which she had born unto Abraham, mocking.

10 Wherefore she said unto Abraham, Cast out this bondwoman and her son: for the son of this bondwoman shall not be heir with my son, *even* with Isaac.

11 And the thing was very grievous in Abraham's sight because of his son.

12 And God said unto Abraham, Let it not be grievous in thy sight because of the lad, and because of thy bondwoman; in all that Sarah hath said unto thee, hearken unto her voice; for in Isaac shall thy seed be called.

13 And also of the son of the bondwoman will I make a nation, because he *is* thy seed.

14 And Abraham rose up early in the morning, and took bread, and a bottle of water, and gave *it* unto Hagar, putting *it* on her shoulder, and the child, and sent her away: and she departed, and wandered in the wilderness of Beersheba.

HANNAH WAS TEASED AND TAUNTED

We ought to bear one another's burdens, not add to them. Hannah could not bear the provocation. Those who are of a fretful spirit, and are apt to lay provocations too much to heart, are enemies to themselves, and strip themselves of many comforts both of life and godliness. We ought to notice comforts, to keep us from grieving for crosses. We should look at that which is for us, as well as what is against us. Hannah mingled tears with her prayers; she considered the mercy of our God, who knows the troubled soul. God gives us leave, in prayer, not only to ask good things in general, but to mention that special good thing we most need and desire. She spoke softly, none could hear her. Hereby she testified her belief of God's knowledge of the heart and its desires. When we are at any time unjustly censured, we have need to set a double watch before the door of our lips, that we do not return censure for censure. Hannah went away with satisfaction of mind. She had herself by prayer committed her case to God, and Eli had prayed for her. Prayer is heart's ease to a gracious soul. Prayer will smooth the countenance; it should do so. None will long remain miserable, who use aright the privilege of going to the mercy-seat of a reconciled God in Christ Jesus.

1 Samuel 1:5-10

But unto Hannah he gave a worthy portion; for he loved Hannah: but the LORD had shut up her womb.

6 And her adversary also provoked her sore, for to make her fret, because the LORD had shut up her womb.

7 And *as* he did so year by year, when she went up to the house of the LORD, so she provoked her; therefore she wept, and did not eat.

8 Then said Elkanah her husband to her, Hannah, why weepest thou? and why eatest thou not? and why is thy heart grieved? *am* not I better to thee than ten sons?

9 So Hannah rose up after they had eaten in Shiloh, and after they had drunk. Now Eli the priest sat upon a seat by a post of the temple of the LORD.

10 And she *was* in bitterness of soul, and prayed unto the LORD, and wept sore.

Hosea Was Commanded To Marry A Prostitute

Hosea is supposed to have been of the kingdom of Israel. He lived and prophesied during a long period. The scope of his predictions appears to be, to detect, reprove, and convince the Jewish nation in general, and the Israelites in particular, of their many sins, particularly their idolatry: the corrupt state of the kingdom is also noticed. But he invites them to repentance, with promises of mercy, and gospel predictions of the future restoration of the Israelites and of the Jews, and their final conversion to Christianity. Israel was prosperous, yet then Hosea boldly tells them of their sins, and foretells their destruction. Men are not to be flattered in sinful ways because they prosper in the world; nor will it last long if they go on still in their trespasses. The prophet must show Israel their sin; show it to be exceedingly hateful. Their idolatry is the sin they are here charged with. Giving that glory to any creature which is due to God alone, is an injury and affront to God; such as for a wife to take a stranger, is to her husband. The Lord, doubtless, had good reasons for giving such a command to the prophet; it would form an affecting picture of the Lord's unmerited goodness and unwearied patience, and of the perverseness and ingratitude of Israel. We should be broken and wearied with half that perverseness from others, with which we try the patience and grieve the Spirit of our God. Let us also be ready to bear any cross the Lord appoints.

Hosea 1:1-3

The word of the LORD that came unto Hosea, the son of Beeri, in the days of Uzziah, Jotham, Ahaz, *and* Hezekiah, kings of Judah, and in the days of Jeroboam the son of Joash, king of Israel.

2 The beginning of the word of the LORD by Hosea. And the LORD said to Hosea, Go, take unto thee a wife of whoredoms and children of whoredoms: for the land hath committed great whoredom, *departing* from the LORD.

3 So he went and took Gomer the daughter of Diblaim; which conceived, and bare him a son.

Jacob Limped

A great while before day, Jacob being alone, more fully spread his fears before God in prayer. While thus employed, One in the likeness of a man wrestled with him. When the spirit helped our infirmities, and our earnest and vast desires can scarcely find words to utter them, and we still mean more than we can express, then prayer is indeed wrestling with God. However tried or discouraged, we shall prevail; and prevailing with Him in prayer, we shall prevail against all enemies that strive with us. Nothing requires more vigor and unceasing exertion than wrestling. It is an emblem of the true spirit of faith and prayer. Jacob kept his ground; though the struggle continued long, this did not shake his faith, nor silence his prayer. He will have a blessing, and had rather have all his bone put out of joint than go away without one. Those who would have the blessing of Christ, must resolve to take no denial. The fervent prayer is the effectual prayer.

Genesis 32:24-32

And Jacob was left alone; and there wrestled a man with him until the breaking of the day.

25 And when he saw that he prevailed not against him, he touched the hollow of his thigh; and the hollow of Jacob's thigh was out of joint, as he wrestled with him.

26 And he said, Let me go, for the day breaketh. And he said, I will not let thee go, except thou bless me.

27 And he said unto him, What *is* thy name? And he said, Jacob.

28 And he said, Thy name shall be called no more Jacob, but Israel: for as a prince hast thou power with God and with men, and hast prevailed.

29 And Jacob asked *him*, and said, Tell *me*, I pray thee, thy name. And

he said, Wherefore *is* it *that* thou dost ask after my name? And he blessed
him there.
30 And Jacob called the name of the place Peniel: for I have seen God
face to face, and my life is preserved.
31 And as he passed over Penuel the sun rose upon him, and he halted
upon his thigh.
32 Therefore the children of Israel eat not *of* the sinew which shrank,
which *is* upon the hollow of the thigh, unto this day: because he touched
the hollow of Jacob's thigh in the sinew that shrank.

Jacob Was A Trickster Until He Discovered His Uncle, Laban, Was A Greater Trickster

During the month that Jacob spent as a guest, he was not idle. Wherever we are, it is good to employ ourselves in some useful business. Laban was desirous that Jacob should continue with him. Inferior relations must not be imposed upon; it is our duty to reward them. Jacob made known to Laban the affection he had for his daughter Rachel. And having no worldly goods with which to endow her, he promises seven years' service Love makes long and hard services short and easy; hence we read of the labor of love. If we know how to value the happiness of heaven, the sufferings of this present time will be as nothing to us. An age of work will be but as a few days to those that love God, and long for Christ's appearing. Jacob, who had imposed upon his father, is imposed upon by Laban, his father-in-law, by a like deception. Herein, how Laban was, the Lord was righteous: see Even the righteous, if they take a false step, are sometimes thus recompensed in the earth. And many who are not, like Jacob, in their marriage, disappointed in person, soon find themselves, as much to their grief, disappointed in the character. The choice of that relation ought to be made with good advice and thought on both sides. There is reason to believe that Laban's excuse was not true. His way of settling the matter made bad worse. Jacob was drawn into the disquiet of multiplying wives. He could not refuse Rachel, for he had espoused her; still less could he refuse Leah. As yet there was no express command against marrying more than one wife. It was in the patriarchs a sin of ignorance; but it will not justify the like practice now, when God's will is plainly made known by the Divine law, and more fully since, by our Savior, that one man and woman only must be joined together,

Genesis 29:25-28

25 And it came to pass, that in the morning, behold, it *was* Leah: and
he said to Laban, What *is* this thou hast done unto me? did not I serve
with thee for Rachel? wherefore then hast thou beguiled me?
26 And Laban said, It must not be so done in our country, to give the
younger before the firstborn.
27 Fulfil her week, and we will give thee this also for the service which
thou shalt serve with me yet seven other years.
28 And Jacob did so, and fulfilled her week: and he gave him Rachel
his daughter to wife also.

Jairus' Daughter Was Sick

The death of our relations should drive us to Christ, who is our life. And it is high honor to the greatest rulers to attend on the Lord Jesus; and those who would receive mercy from Christ, must honor him. The variety of methods Christ took in working his miracles, perhaps was because of the different frames and tempers of mind, which those were in who came to him, and which He who searches the heart perfectly knew. A poor woman applied herself to Christ, and received mercy from him by the way. If we do but touch, as it were, the hem of Christ's garment by living faith, our worst evils will be healed; there is no other real cure, nor need we fear his knowing things which are a grief and burden to us, but which we would not tell any earthly friend. When Christ entered the ruler's house, he said, Give place. Sometimes, when the sorrow of the world prevails, it is difficult for Christ and his comforts to enter. The ruler's daughter was really dead, but not so to Christ. The death of the righteous is in a special manner to be looked on as only a sleep. The words and works of Christ may not at first be understood, yet they are not therefore to be despised. The people were put forth. Scorners who laugh at what they do not understand, are not proper witnesses of the wonderful works of Christ. Dead souls are not raised to spiritual life, unless Christ take them by the hand: it is done in the day of his power. If this single instance of Christ's raising one newly dead so increased his fame, what will be his glory when all that are in their graves shall hear his voice, and come forth; those that have done good to the resurrection of life, and those that have done evil to the resurrection of damnation!

Matthew 9:18-19, 23-25

18While he spake these things unto them, behold, there came a certain
ruler, and worshipped him, saying, My daughter is even now dead: but
come and lay thy hand upon her, and she shall live.
19 And Jesus arose, and followed him, and *so did* his disciples.
23 And when Jesus came into the ruler's house, and saw the minstrels
and the people making a noise,
24 He said unto them, Give place: for the maid is not dead, but
sleepeth. And they laughed him to scorn.
25 But when the people were put forth, he went in, and took her by
the hand, and the maid arose.

Jephthah Made A Stupid Vow And Had To Sacrifice His Only Daughter

Several important lessons are to be learned from Jephthah's vow. 1. There may be remainders of distrust and doubting, even in the hearts of true and great believers. 2. Our vows to God should not be as a purchase of the favor we desire, but to express gratitude to him. 3. We need to be very well-advised in making vows, lest we entangle ourselves. 4. What we have solemnly vowed to God, we must perform, if it be possible and lawful, though it be difficult and grievous to us. 5. It well becomes children, obediently and cheerfully to submit to their parents in the Lord. It is hard to say what Jephthah did in performance of his vow; but it is thought that he did not offer his daughter as a burnt-offering. Such a sacrifice would have been an abomination to the Lord; it is supposed she was obliged to remain unmarried, and apart from her family. Concerning this and some other such passages in the sacred history, about which learned men are divided and in doubt, we need not perplex ourselves; what is necessary to our salvation, thanks be to God, is plain enough. If the reader recollects the promise of Christ concerning the teaching of the Holy Spirit, and places himself under this heavenly Teacher, the Holy Ghost will guide to all truth in every passage, so far as it is needful to be understood.

Judges 11:30-35

And Jephthah vowed a vow unto the LORD, and said, If thou shalt without fail deliver the children of Ammon into mine hands,

31 Then it shall be, that whatsoever cometh forth of the doors of my house to meet me, when I return in peace from the children of Ammon, shall surely be the LORD'S, and I will offer it up for a burnt offering.

32 So Jephthah passed over unto the children of Ammon to fight against them; and the LORD delivered them into his hands.

33 And he smote them from Aroer, even till thou come to Minnith, *even* twenty cities, and unto the plain of the vineyards, with a very great slaughter. Thus the children of Ammon were subdued before the children of Israel.

34 And Jephthah came to Mizpeh unto his house, and, behold, his daughter came out to meet him with timbrels and with dances: and she *was his* only child; beside her he had neither son nor daughter.

35 And it came to pass, when he saw her, that he rent his clothes, and said, Alas, my daughter! thou hast brought me very low, and thou art one of them that trouble me: for I have opened my mouth unto the LORD, and I cannot go back.

Jeremiah Was Put Down A Well

Jeremiah is cast into a dungeon, from whence he is delivered by an Ethiopian. He advises the king to surrender to the Chaldeans. Jeremiah went on in his plain preaching. The princes went on in their malice. It is common for wicked people to look upon God's faithful ministers as enemies, because they show what enemies the wicked are to themselves while impenitent. Jeremiah was put into a dungeon. Many of God's faithful witnesses have been privately made away in prisons. Ebed-melech was an Ethiopian; yet he spoke to the king faithfully., These men have done ill in all they have done to Jeremiah. See how God can raise up friends for his people in distress. Orders were given for the prophet's release, and Ebed-melech saw him drawn up. Let this encourage us to appear boldly for God. Special notice is taken of his tenderness for Jeremiah. What do we behold in the different characters then, but the same we behold in the different characters now, that the Lord's children are conformed to his example, and the children of Satan to their master?

Jeremiah 38:6-13

Then took they Jeremiah, and cast him into the dungeon of Malchiah the son of Hammelech, that *was* in the court of the prison: and they let down Jeremiah with cords. And in the dungeon *there was* no water, but mire: so Jeremiah sunk in the mire.

7 Now when Ebedmelech the Ethiopian, one of the eunuchs which was in the king's house, heard that they had put Jeremiah in the dungeon; the king then sitting in the gate of Benjamin;

8 Ebedmelech went forth out of the king's house, and spake to the king, saying,

9 My lord the king, these men have done evil in all that they have done to Jeremiah the prophet, whom they have cast into the dungeon; and he is like to die for hunger in the place where he is: for *there is* no more bread in the city.

10 Then the king commanded Ebedmelech the Ethiopian, saying, Take from hence thirty men with thee, and take up Jeremiah the prophet out of the dungeon, before he die.

11 So Ebedmelech took the men with him, and went into the house of the king under the treasury, and took thence old cast clouts and old rotten rags, and let them down by cords into the dungeon to Jeremiah.

12 And Ebedmelech the Ethiopian said unto Jeremiah, Put now *these* old cast clouts and rotten rags under thine armholes under the cords. And Jeremiah did so.

13 So they drew up Jeremiah with cords, and took him up out of the dungeon: and Jeremiah remained in the court of the prison.

Jeremiah Was The Weeping Prophet

Jeremiah wept much, yet wished he could weep more, that he might rouse the people to a due sense of the hand of God. But even the desert, without communion with God, through Christ Jesus, and the influences of the Holy Spirit, must be a place for temptation and evil; while, with these blessings, we may live in holiness in crowded cities. The people accustomed their tongues to lies. So false were they, that a brother could not be trusted. In trading and bargaining they said anything for their own advantage, though they knew it to be false. But God marked their sin. Where no knowledge of God is, what good can be expected? He has many ways of turning a fruitful land into barrenness for the wickedness of those that dwell therein.

Jeremiah 9:1

Oh that my head were waters, and mine eyes a fountain of tears, that I might weep day and night for the slain of the daughter of my people!

Jesus Was Crucified On A Cross

Wicked men see little of the consequences of their crimes when they commit them, but they must answer for them all. In the fullest manner Judas acknowledged to the chief priests that he had sinned, and betrayed an innocent person. This was full testimony to the character of Christ; but the rulers were hardened. Casting down the money, Judas departed, and went and hanged himself, not being able to bear the terror of Divine wrath, and the anguish of despair. There is little doubt but that the death of Judas was before that of our blessed Lord. But was it nothing to them that they had thirsted after this blood, and hired Judas to betray it, and had condemned it to be shed unjustly? Thus, do fools make a mock at sin. Thus, many make light of Christ crucified. And it is a common instance of the deceitfulness of our hearts, to make light of our own sin by dwelling upon other people's sins. But the judgment of God is according to truth. Many apply this passage of the buying the piece of ground, with the money Judas brought back, to signify the favor intended by the blood of Christ to strangers, and sinners of the Gentiles. It fulfilled a prophecy. Judas went far toward repentance, yet it was not to salvation. He confessed, but not to God; he did not go to him, and say, I have sinned, Father, against heaven. Let none be satisfied with such partial convictions as a man may have, and yet remain full of pride, enmity, and rebellion. Having no malice against Jesus, Pilate urged him to clear himself, and labored to get him discharged. The message from his wife was a warning. God has many ways of giving checks to sinners, in their sinful pursuits, and it is a great mercy to have such checks from Providence, from faithful friends, and from our own consciences. O do not this abominable thing which the Lord hates! is what we may hear said to us, when we are entering into temptation, if we will but regard it. Being overruled by the priests, the people made choice of Barabbas. Multitudes who choose the world, rather than God, for their ruler and portion, thus choose their own delusions. The Jews were so bent upon the death of Christ, that Pilate thought it would be dangerous to refuse. And this struggle shows the power of conscience even on the worst men. Yet all was so ordered to make it evident that Christ suffered for no fault of his own, but for the sins of his people. How vain for Pilate to expect to free himself from the guilt of the innocent blood of a righteous person, whom he was by his office bound to protect! The Jews' curse upon themselves has been awfully answered in the sufferings of their nation. None could bear the sin of others, except Him that had no sin of his own to answer for. And are we not all concerned? Is not Barabbas preferred to Jesus, when sinners reject salvation that they may retain their darling sins, which rob God of his glory, and murder their souls? The blood of Christ is now upon us for good, through mercy, by the Jews' rejection of it. O let us flee to it for refuge! Crucifixion was a death used only among the Romans; it was very terrible and miserable. A cross was laid on the ground, to which the hands and feet were nailed, it was then lifted up and fixed upright, so that the weight of the body hung on the nails, till the sufferer died in agony. Christ thus answered the type of the brazen serpent raised on a pole. Christ underwent all the misery and shame here related, that he might purchase for us everlasting life, and joy, and glory.

Christ was led as a Lamb to the slaughter, as a Sacrifice to the altar. Even the mercies of the wicked are really cruel. Taking the cross from him, they compelled one Simon to bear it. Make us ready, O Lord, to bear the cross thou hast appointed us, and daily to take it up with cheerfulness, following thee. Was ever sorrow like unto his sorrow? And when we behold what manner of death he died, let us in that behold with what manner of love he loved us. As if death, so painful a death, were not enough, they added to its bitterness and terror in several ways. It was usual to put shame upon malefactors, by a writing to notify the crime for which they suffered. So, they set up one over Christ's head. This they designed for his reproach, but God so overruled it, that even his accusation was to his honor. There were crucified with him at the same time, two robbers. He was, at his death, numbered among the transgressors, that we, at our death, might be numbered among the saints. The taunts and jeers he received are here recorded. The enemies of Christ labor to make others believe that of religion and of the people of God, which they themselves know to be false.

The chief priests and scribes, and the elders, upbraid Jesus with being the King of Israel. Many people could like the King of Israel well enough, if he would but come down from the cross; if they could but have his kingdom without the tribulation through which they must enter into it. But if no cross, then no Christ, no crown. Those that would reign with him, must be willing to suffer with him. Thus, our Lord Jesus, having undertaken to satisfy the justice of God, did it, by submitting to the punishment of the worst of men. And in every minute particular recorded about the sufferings of Christ, we find some prediction in the Prophets or the Psalms fulfilled. During the three hours which the darkness continued, Jesus was in agony, wrestling with the powers of darkness, and suffering his Father's displeasure against the sin of man, for which he was now making his soul an offering. Never were there three such hours since the day God created man upon the earth, never such a dark and awful scene; it was the turning point of that great affair, man's redemption and salvation. Jesus uttered a complaint from. Hereby he teaches of what use the word of God is to direct us in prayer, and recommends the use of Scripture expressions in prayer. The believer may have tasted some drops of bitterness, but he can only form a very feeble idea of the greatness of Christ's sufferings. Yet, hence he learns something of the Savior's love to sinners; hence he gets deeper conviction of the vileness and evil of sin, and of what he owes to Christ, who delivers him from the wrath to come. His enemies wickedly ridiculed his complaint. Many of the reproaches cast upon the word of God and the people of God, arise, as here, from gross mistakes. Christ, just before he expired, spake in his full strength, to show that his life was not forced from him, but was freely delivered into his Father's hands. He had strength to bid defiance to the powers of death: and to show that by the eternal Spirit he offered himself, being the Priest as well as the Sacrifice, he cried with a loud voice. Then he yielded up the ghost. The Son of God upon the cross, did die by the violence of the pain he was put to. His soul was separated from his body, and so his body was left really and truly dead. It was certain that Christ did die, for it was needful that he should die. He had undertaken to make himself an offering for sin, and he did it when he willingly gave up his life.

Matthew 27:35-50

35 And they crucified him, and parted his garments, casting lots: that it might be fulfilled which was spoken by the prophet, They parted my garments among them, and upon my vesture did they cast lots.

36 And sitting down they watched him there;

37 And set up over his head his accusation written, THIS IS JESUS THE KING OF THE JEWS.

38 Then were there two thieves crucified with him, one on the right hand, and another on the left.

39 And they that passed by reviled him, wagging their heads,

40 And saying, Thou that destroyest the temple, and buildest *it* in three days, save thyself. If thou be the Son of God, come down from the cross.

41 Likewise also the chief priests mocking *him*, with the scribes and elders, said,

42 He saved others; himself he cannot save. If he be the King of Israel, let him now come down from the cross, and we will believe him.

43 He trusted in God; let him deliver him now, if he will have him: for he said, I am the Son of God.

44 The thieves also, which were crucified with him, cast the same in his teeth.

45 Now from the sixth hour there was darkness over all the land unto the ninth hour.

46 And about the ninth hour Jesus cried with a loud voice, saying, Eli, Eli, lama sabachthani? that is to say, My God, my God, why hast thou forsaken me?

47 Some of them that stood there, when they heard *that*, said, This *man* calleth for Elias.

48 And straightway one of them ran, and took a spunge, and filled *it* with vinegar, and put *it* on a reed, and gave him to drink.

49 The rest said, Let be, let us see whether Elias will come to save him.

50 Jesus, when he had cried again with a loud voice, yielded up the ghost.

Jezebel Was Wicked. When She Died The Dogs Ate Up Her Body Except Her Skull, The Palm Of Her Hands And The Soles Of Her Feet

Jehu was a man of eager spirit. The wisdom of God is seen in the choice of those employed in his work. But it is not for any man's reputation to be known by his fury. He that has rule over his own spirit, is better than the mighty. Joram met Jehu in the portion of Naboth. The circumstances of events are sometimes ordered by Divine Providence to make the punishment answer to the sin, as face answers to face in a glass. The way of sin can never be the way of peace. What peace can sinners have with God? No peace so long as sin is persisted in; but when it is repented of and forsaken, there is peace. Joram died as a criminal, under the sentence of the law. Ahaziah was joined with the house of Ahab. He was one of them; he had made himself so by sin. It is dangerous to join evil-doers; we shall be entangled in guilt and misery by it.

Instead of hiding herself, as one afraid of Divine vengeance, Jezebel mocked at fear. See how a heart, hardened against God, will brave it out to the last. There is not a surer presage of ruin, than an unhumble heart under humbling providences. Let those look at Jezebel's conduct and fate, who use arts to seduce others to commit wickedness, and to draw them aside from the ways of truth and righteousness. Jehu called for aid against Jezebel. When reformation-work is on foot, it is time to ask, Who sides with it? Her attendants delivered her up. Thus, she was put to death. See the end of pride and cruelty, and say, The Lord is righteous. When we pamper our bodies, let us think how vile they are; shortly they will be a feast for worms underground, or beasts above ground. May we all flee from that wrath which is revealed from heaven, against all ungodliness and unrighteousness of men.

2 Kings 9:33-37

33 And he said, Throw her down. So they threw her down: and *some* of her blood was sprinkled on the wall, and on the horses: and he trode her under foot.

34 And when he was come in, he did eat and drink, and said, Go, see now this cursed *woman*, and bury her: for she *is* a king's daughter.

35 And they went to bury her: but they found no more of her than the skull, and the feet, and the palms of *her* hands.

36 Wherefore they came again, and told him. And he said, This *is* the word of the LORD, which he spake by his servant Elijah the Tishbite, saying, In the portion of Jezreel shall dogs eat the flesh of Jezebel:

37 And the carcase of Jezebel shall be as dung upon the face of the field in the portion of Jezreel; *so* that they shall not say, This *is* Jezebel.

Job Lost All His Wealth, Ten Children And Was Afflicted With Sores All On The Same Day

Satan brought Job's troubles upon him on the day that his children began their course of feasting. The troubles all came upon Job at once; while one messenger of evil tidings was speaking, another followed. His dearest and most valuable possessions were his ten children; news has brought him that they are killed. They were taken away when he had most need of them to comfort him under other losses. In God only have we a help present at all times.

Job humbled himself under the hand of God. He reasons from the common state of human life, which he describes. We brought nothing of this world's goods into the world, but have them from others; and it is certain we can carry nothing out, but must leave them to others. Job, under all his losses, is but reduced to his first state. He is but where he must have been at last, and is only unclothed, or unloaded rather, a little sooner than he expected. If we put off our clothes before we go to bed, it is some inconvenience, but it may be the better borne when it is near bed-time. The same who gave hath taken away. See how Job looks above instruments, and keeps his eye upon the First Cause. Afflictions must not divert us from, but quicken us to religion. If in all our troubles we look to the Lord, he will support us. The Lord is righteous. All we have is from his gift; we have forfeited it by sin, and ought not to complain if he takes any part from us. Discontent and impatience charge God with folly. Against these Job carefully watched; and so, must we, acknowledging that as God has done right, but we have done wickedly, so God has done wisely, but we have done very foolishly. And may the malice and power of Satan render that Savior more precious to our souls, who came to destroy the works of the devil; who, for our salvation, suffered from that enemy far more than Job suffered, or we can think.

Job 1: 13-22 Joseph Lost all His Wealth and Ten Children

And there was a day when his sons and his daughters *were* eating and drinking wine in their eldest brother's house:

14 And there came a messenger unto Job, and said, The oxen were plowing, and the asses feeding beside them:

15 And the Sabeans fell *upon them*, and took them away; yea, they have slain the servants with the edge of the sword; and I only am escaped alone to tell thee.

16 While he *was* yet speaking, there came also another, and said, The fire of God is fallen from heaven, and hath burned up the sheep, and the servants, and consumed them; and I only am escaped alone to tell thee.

17 While he *was* yet speaking, there came also another, and said, The Chaldeans made out three bands, and fell upon the camels, and have carried them away, yea, and slain the servants with the edge of the sword; and I only am escaped alone to tell thee.

18 While he *was* yet speaking, there came also another, and said, Thy sons and thy daughters *were* eating and drinking wine in their eldest brother's house:

19 And, behold, there came a great wind from the wilderness, and smote the four corners of the house, and it fell upon the young men, and they are dead; and I only am escaped alone to tell thee.

20 Then Job arose, and rent his mantle, and shaved his head, and fell down upon the ground, and worshipped,

21 And said, Naked came I out of my mother's womb, and naked shall I return thither: the LORD gave, and the LORD hath taken away; blessed be the name of the LORD.

22 In all this Job sinned not, nor charged God foolishly

How well is it for us, that neither men nor devils are to be our judges! but all our judgment comes from the Lord, who never errs. Job holds fast his integrity still, as his weapon. God speaks with pleasure of the power of his own grace. Self-love and self-preservation are powerful in the hearts of men. But Satan accuses Job, representing him as wholly selfish, and minding nothing but his own ease and safety. Thus, are the ways and people of God often falsely blamed by the devil and his agents. Permission is granted to Satan to make trial, but with a limit. If God did not chain up the roaring lion, how soon would he devour us! Job, thus slandered by Satan, was a type of Christ, the first prophecy of whom was, that Satan should bruise his heel, and be foiled.

The devil tempts his own children, and draws them to sin, and afterwards torments, when he has brought them to ruin; but this child of God he tormented with affliction, and then tempted to make a bad use of his affliction. He provoked Job to curse God. The disease was very grievous. If at any time we are tried with sore and grievous distempers, let us not think ourselves dealt with otherwise than as God sometimes deals with the best of his saints and servants. Job humbled himself under the mighty hand of God, and brought his mind to his condition. His wife was spared to him, to be a troubler and tempter to him. Satan still endeavors to draw men from God, as he did our first parents, by suggesting hard thoughts of Him, then which nothing is falser. But Job resisted and overcame the temptation. Shall we, guilty, polluted, worthless creatures, receive so many unmerited blessings from a just and holy God, and shall we refuse to accept the punishment of our sins, when we suffer so much less than we deserve? Let murmuring, as well as boasting, be for ever done away. Thus far Job stood the trial, and appeared brightest in the furnace of affliction. There might be risings of corruption in his heart, but grace had the upper hand.

Job 2: 1-7 Josephs' Body Covered with Boils

Again there was a day when the sons of God came to present themselves before the LORD, and Satan came also among them to present himself before the LORD.

2 And the LORD said unto Satan, From whence comest thou? And Satan answered the LORD, and said, From going to and fro in the earth, and from walking up and down in it.

3 And the LORD said unto Satan, Hast thou considered my servant

Job, that *there is* none like him in the earth, a perfect and an upright man, one that feareth God, and escheweth evil? and still he holdeth fast his integrity, although thou movedst me against him, to destroy him without cause.

4 And Satan answered the LORD, and said, Skin for skin, yea, all that
a man hath will he give for his life.

5 But put forth thine hand now, and touch his bone and his flesh, and
he will curse thee to thy face.

6 And the LORD said unto Satan, Behold, he *is* in thine hand; but
save his life.

7 So went Satan forth from the presence of the LORD, and smote Job
with sore boils from the sole of his foot unto his crown

John The Baptist Was Beheaded

Herod feared John while he lived, and feared him still more when he was dead. Herod did many of those things which John in his preaching taught him; but it is not enough to do many things, we must have respect to all the commandments. Herod respected John, till he touched him in his Herodias. Thus, many love good preaching, if it keeps far away from their beloved sin. But it is better that sinners persecute ministers now for faithfulness, then curse them eternally for unfaithfulness. The ways of God are unsearchable; but we may be sure he never can be at a loss to repay his servants for what they endure or lose for his sake. Death could not come so as to surprise this holy man; and the triumph of the wicked was short.

Mark 6: 23-28

23 And he sware unto her, Whatsoever thou shalt ask of me, I will give *it* thee, unto the half of my kingdom.

24 And she went forth, and said unto her mother, What shall I ask? And she said, The head of John the Baptist.

25 And she came in straightway with haste unto the king, and asked, saying, I will that thou give me by and by in a charger the head of John the Baptist.

26 And the king was exceeding sorry; *yet* for his oath's sake, and for their sakes which sat with him, he would not reject her.

27 And immediately the king sent an executioner, and commanded his head to be brought: and he went and beheaded him in the prison,

28 And brought his head in a charger, and gave it to the damsel: and the damsel gave it to her mother.

John Was Banished To The Isle Of Patmos

It was the apostle's comfort that he did not suffer as an evil-doer, but for the testimony of Jesus, for bearing witness to Christ as the Immanuel, the Saviour; and the Spirit of glory and of God rested upon this persecuted apostle. The day and time when he had this vision was the Lord's day, the Christian sabbath, the first day of the week, observed in remembrance of the resurrection of Christ. Let us who call him "Our Lord," honour him on his own day. The name shows how this sacred day should be observed; the Lord's day should be wholly devoted to the Lord, and none of its hours employed in a sensual, worldly manner, or in amusements. He was in a serious, heavenly, spiritual frame, under the gracious influences of the Spirit of God. Those who would enjoy communion with God on the Lord's day, must seek to draw their thoughts and affections from earthly things. And if believers are kept on the Lord's holy day, from public ordinances and the communion of saints, by necessity and not by choice, they may look for comfort in meditation and secret duties, from the influences of the Spirit; and by hearing the voice and contemplating the glory of their beloved Saviour, from whose gracious words and power no confinement or outward circumstances can separate them. An alarm was given as with the sound of the trumpet, and then the apostle heard the voice of Christ.

Revelation 1:8-11

8 I am Alpha and Omega, the beginning and the ending, saith the Lord, which is, and which was, and which is to come, the Almighty.

9 I John, who also am your brother, and companion in tribulation, and in the kingdom and patience of Jesus Christ, was in the isle that is called Patmos, for the word of God, and for the testimony of Jesus Christ.

10 I was in the Spirit on the Lord's day, and heard behind me a great voice, as of a trumpet,

11 Saying, I am Alpha and Omega, the first and the last: and, What thou seest, write in a book, and send *it* unto the seven churches which are in Asia; unto Ephesus, and unto Smyrna, and unto Pergamos, and unto Thyatira, and unto Sardis, and unto Philadelphia, and unto Laodicea.

Jonah Pouted

Jonah repines at God's mercy to Nineveh, and is reproved. He is taught by the withering of a gourd, that he did wrong. What all the saints make matter of joy and praise, Jonah makes the subject of reflection upon God; as if showing mercy were an imperfection of the Divine nature, which is the greatest glory of it. It is to his sparing, pardoning mercy, we all owe it that we are out of hell. He wishes for death: this was the language of folly, passion, and strong corruption. There appeared in Jonah remains of a proud, uncharitable spirit; and that he neither expected nor desired the welfare of the Ninevites, but had only come to declare and witness their destruction. He was not duly humbled for his own sins, and was not willing to trust the Lord with his credit and safety. In this frame of mind, he overlooked the good of which he had been an instrument, and the glory of the Divine mercy. We should often ask ourselves, Is it well to say thus, to do this? Can I justify it? Do I well to be so soon angry, so often angry, so long angry, and to give others ill language in my anger? Do I well to be angry at the mercy of God to repenting sinners? That was Jonah's crime. Do we do well to be angry at that which is for the glory of God, and the advancement of his kingdom? Let the conversion of sinners, which is the joy of heaven, be our joy, and never our grief.

Jonah went out of the city, yet remained near at hand, as if he expected and desired its overthrow. Those who have fretful, uneasy spirits, often make troubles for themselves, that they may still have something to complain of. See how tender God is of his people in their afflictions, even though they are foolish and froward. A thing small in itself, yet coming seasonably, may be a valuable blessing. A gourd in the right place may do us more service than a cedar. The least creatures may be great plagues, or great comforts, as God is pleased to make them. Persons of strong passions are apt to be cast down with any trifle that crosses them, or to be lifted up with a trifle that pleases them. See what our creature-comforts are, and what we may expect them to be; they are withering things. Perhaps creature-comforts are continued to us, but are made bitter; the creature is continued, but the comfort is gone. God prepared a wind to make Jonah feel the want of the gourd. It is just that those who love to complain, should never be left without something to complain of. When afflicting providences take away relations, possessions, and enjoyments, we must not be angry at God. What should especially silence discontent, is, that when our gourd is gone, our God is not gone. Sin and death are very dreadful, yet Jonah, in his heat, makes light of both. One soul is of more value than the whole world; surely then one soul is of more value than many gourds: we should have more concern for our own and others' precious souls, than for the riches and enjoyments of this world. It is a great encouragement to hope we shall find mercy with the Lord, that he is ready to show mercy. And murmurers shall be made to understand, that how willing they are to keep the Divine grace to themselves and those of their own way, there is one Lord over all, who is rich in mercy to all that call upon him. Do we wonder at the forbearance of God towards his perverse servant? Let us study our own hearts and ways; let us not forget our own ingratitude and obstinacy; and let us be astonished at God's patience towards us.

Jonah 4:1-4

But it displeased Jonah exceedingly, and he was very angry.

2 And he prayed unto the LORD, and said, I pray thee, O LORD, *was* not this my saying, when I was yet in my country? Therefore I fled before unto Tarshish: for I knew that thou *art* a gracious God, and merciful, slow to anger, and of great kindness, and repentest thee of the evil.

3 Therefore now, O LORD, take, I beseech thee, my life from me; for *it is* better for me to die than to live.

4 Then said the LORD, Doest thou well to be angry?

Joseph Was Sold Into Slavery

Joseph is loved of Jacob, but hated by his brethren. Joseph's dreams. Jacob sends Joseph to visit his brethren, They conspire his death. Joseph's brethren sell him. Jacob deceived, Joseph sold to Potiphar. Joseph's history we see something of Christ, who was first humbled and then exalted. It also shows the lot of Christians, who must through many tribulations enter into the kingdom. It is a history that has none like it, for displaying the various workings of the human mind, both good and bad, and the singular providence of God in making use of them for fulfilling his purposes. Though Joseph was his father's darling, yet he was not bred up in idleness. Those do not truly love their children, who do not use them to business, and labor, and hardships. The fondling of children is with good reason called the spoiling of them. Those who are trained up to do nothing, are likely to be good for nothing. But Jacob made known his love, by dressing Joseph finer than the rest of his children. It is wrong for parents to make a difference between one child and another, unless there is great cause for it, by the children's dutifulness, or undutifulness. When parents make a difference, children soon notice it, and it leads to quarrels in families. Jacob's sons did that, when they were from under his eye, which they durst not have done at home with him; but Joseph gave his father an account of their ill conduct, that he might restrain them. Not as a tale-bearer, to sow discord, but as a faithful brother. God gave Joseph betimes the prospect of his advancement, to support and comfort him under his long and grievous troubles. Observe, Joseph dreamed of his preferment, but he did not dream of his imprisonment. Thus, many young people, when setting out in the world, think of nothing but prosperity and pleasure, and never dream of trouble. His brethren rightly interpreted the dream, though they abhorred the interpretation of it. While they committed crimes in order to defeat it, they were themselves the instruments of accomplishing it. Thus, the Jews understood what Christ said of his kingdom. Determined that he should not reign over them, they consulted to put him to death; and by his crucifixion, made way for the exaltation they designed to prevent. How readily does Joseph wait his father's orders! Those children who are best beloved by their parents, should be the readiest to obey them. See how deliberate Joseph's brethren were against him. They thought to slay him from malice aforethought, and in cold blood. Whosoever hated his brother is a murderer|. The sons of Jacob hated their brother because their father loved him. New occasions, as his dreams and the like, drew them on further; but this laid rankling in their hearts, till they resolved on his death. God has all hearts in his hands. Reuben had most reason to be jealous of Joseph, for he was the first-born; yet he proves his best friend. God overruled all to serve his own purpose, of making Joseph an instrument to save much people alive. Joseph was a type of Christ; for though he was the beloved Son of his Father, and hated by a wicked world, yet the Father sent him out of his bosom to visit us in great humility and love. He came from heaven to earth to seek and save us; yet then malicious plots were laid against him. His own not only received him not, but crucified him. This he submitted to, as a part of his design to redeem and save us. They threw Joseph into a pit, to perish there with hunger and cold; so cruel were their tender mercies. They slighted him when he was in distress, and were not grieved for the affliction of Joseph, for when he was pining in the pit, they sat down to eat bread. They felt no remorse of conscience for the sin. But the wrath of man shall praise God, and the remainder of wrath he will restrain. Joseph's brethren were wonderfully restrained from murdering him, and their selling him as wonderfully turned to God's praise.

Genesis 37:23-28

23 And it came to pass, when Joseph was come unto his brethren, that they stript Joseph out of his coat, *his* coat of *many* colours that *was* on him;

24 And they took him, and cast him into a pit: and the pit *was* empty, *there was* no water in it.

25 And they sat down to eat bread: and they lifted up their eyes and looked, and, behold, a company of Ishmeelites came from Gilead with their camels bearing spicery and balm and myrrh, going to carry *it* down to Egypt.

26 And Judah said unto his brethren, What profit *is it* if we slay our brother, and conceal his blood?

27 Come, and let us sell him to the Ishmeelites, and let not our hand be upon him; for he *is* our brother *and* our flesh. And his brethren were content.

28 Then there passed by Midianites merchantmen; and they drew and lifted up Joseph out of the pit, and sold Joseph to the Ishmeelites for twenty *pieces* of silver: and they brought Joseph into Egypt

Judas Killed Himself

Wicked men see little of the consequences of their crimes when they commit them, but they must answer for them all. In the fullest manner Judas acknowledged to the chief priests that he had sinned, and betrayed an innocent person. This was full testimony to the character of Christ; but the rulers were hardened. Casting down the money, Judas departed, and went and hanged himself, not being able to bear the terror of Divine wrath, and the anguish of despair. There is little doubt but that the death of Judas was before that of our blessed Lord. But was it nothing to them that they had thirsted after this blood, and hired Judas to betray it, and had condemned it to be shed unjustly? Thus, do fools make a mock at sin. Thus, many make light of Christ crucified. And it is a common instance of the deceitfulness of our hearts, to make light of our own sin by dwelling upon other people's sins. But the judgment of God is according to truth. Many apply this passage of the buying the piece of ground, with the money Judas brought back, to signify the favor intended by the blood of Christ to strangers, and sinners of the Gentiles. It fulfilled a prophecy. Judas went far toward repentance, yet it was not to salvation. He confessed, but not to God; he did not go to him, and say, I have sinned, Father, against heaven. Let none be satisfied with such partial convictions as a man may have, and yet remain full of pride, enmity, and rebellion.

Matthew 27:3-5

3 Then Judas, which had betrayed him, when he saw that he was condemned, repented himself, and brought again the thirty pieces of silver to the chief priests and elders,

4 Saying, I have sinned in that I have betrayed the innocent blood.
And they said, What *is that* to us? see thou *to that*.
5 And he cast down the pieces of silver in the temple, and departed,
and went and hanged himself.

Lazarus Died And Was Stinking Before Jesus Brought Him Back To Life

Christ's tender sympathy with these afflicted friends, appeared by the troubles of his spirit. In all the afflictions of believers he is afflicted. His concern for them was shown by his kind inquiry after the remains of his deceased friend. Being found in fashion as a man, he acts in the way and manner of the sons of men. It was shown by his tears. He was a man of sorrows, and acquainted with grief. Tears of compassion resemble those of Christ. But Christ never approved that sensibility of which many are proud, while they weep at mere tales of distress, but are hardened to real woe. He sets us an example to withdraw from scenes of giddy mirth, that we may comfort the afflicted. And we have not a High Priest who cannot be touched with a feeling of our infirmities. It is a good step toward raising a soul to spiritual life, when the stone is taken away, when prejudices are removed, and got over, and way is made for the word to enter the heart. If we take Christ's word, and rely on his power and faithfulness, we shall see the glory of God, and be happy in the sight. Our Lord Jesus has taught us, by his own example, to call God Father, in prayer, and to draw nigh to him as children to a father, with humble reverence, yet with holy boldness. He openly made this address to God, with uplifted eyes and loud voice, that they might be convinced the Father had sent him as his beloved Son into the world. He could have raised Lazarus by the silent exertion of his power and will, and the unseen working of the Spirit of life; but he did it by a loud call. This was a figure of the gospel call, by which dead souls are brought out of the grave of sin: and of the sound of the archangel's trumpet at the last day, with which all that sleep in the dust shall be awakened, and summoned before the great tribunal. The grave of sin and this world is no place for those whom Christ has quickened; they must come forth. Lazarus was thoroughly revived, and returned not only to life, but to health. The sinner cannot quicken his own soul, but he is to use the means of grace; the believer cannot sanctify himself, but he is to lay aside every weight and hinderance. We cannot convert our relatives and friends, but we should instruct, warn, and invite them.

John 11:39-44

39 Jesus said, Take ye away the stone. Martha, the sister of him that was dead, saith unto him, Lord, by this time he stinketh: for he hath been *dead* four days.

40 Jesus saith unto her, Said I not unto thee, that, if thou wouldest believe, thou shouldest see the glory of God?

41 Then they took away the stone *from the place* where the dead was laid. And Jesus lifted up *his* eyes, and said, Father, I thank thee that thou hast heard me.

42 And I knew that thou hearest me always: but because of the people which stand by I said *it*, that they may believe that thou hast sent me.

43 And when he thus had spoken, he cried with a loud voice, Lazarus, come forth.

44 And he that was dead came forth, bound hand and foot with graveclothes: and his face was bound about with a napkin. Jesus saith unto them, Loose him, and let him go.

Leah Had Weak Eyes

And having no worldly goods with which to endow her, he promises seven years' service Love makes long and hard services short and easy; hence we read of the labor of love. If we know how to value the happiness of heaven, the sufferings of this present time will be as nothing to us. An age of work will be but as a few days to those that love God, and long for Christ's appearing. Jacob, who had imposed upon his father, is imposed upon by Laban, his father-in-law, by a like deception. Herein, how unrighteous Laban was, the Lord was righteous: Even the righteous, if they take a false step, are sometimes thus recompensed in the earth. And many who are not, like Jacob, in their marriage, disappointed in person, soon find themselves, as much to their grief, disappointed in the character. The choice of that relation ought to be made with good advice and thought on both sides. There is reason to believe that Laban's excuse was not true. His way of settling the matter made bad worse. Jacob was drawn into the disquiet of multiplying wives. He could not refuse Rachel, for he had espoused her; still less could he refuse Leah. As yet there was no express command against marrying more than one wife. It was in the patriarchs a sin of ignorance; but it will not justify the like practice now, when God's will is plainly made known by the Divine law and more fully since, by our Saviour, that one man and woman only must be joined together'

Genesis 29:16-17

16 And Laban had two daughters: the name of the elder *was* Leah, and the name of the younger *was* Rachel.

17 Leah *was* tender eyed; but Rachel was beautiful and well favoured.

Lot's Wife Turned To A Pillar Of Salt

The destruction of Sodom, and the deliverance of Lot. The sin and disgrace of Lot. Lot was good, but there was not one more of the same character in the city. All the people of Sodom were very wicked and vile. Care was therefore taken for saving Lot and his family. Lot lingered; he trifled. Thus, many who are under convictions about their spiritual state, and the necessity of a change, defer that needful work. The salvation of the most righteous men is of God's mercy, not by their own merit. We are saved by grace. God's power also must be acknowledged in bringing souls out of a sinful state If God had not been merciful to us, our lingering had been our ruin. Lot must flee for his life. He must not hanker after Sodom. Such commands as these are given to those who, through grace, are delivered out of a sinful state and condition. Return not to sin and Satan. Rest not in self and the world. Reach toward Christ and heaven, for that is escaping to the mountain, short of which we must not stop. Concerning this destruction, observe that it is a revelation of the wrath of God against sin and sinners of all ages. Let us learn from hence the evil of sin, and its hurtful nature; it leads to ruin.

Genesis 19:17, 25-26

17 And it came to pass, when they had brought them forth abroad, that he said, Escape for thy life; look not behind thee, neither stay thou in all the plain; escape to the mountain, lest thou be consumed.

25 And he overthrew those cities, and all the plain, and all the inhabitants of the cities, and that which grew upon the ground.

26 But his wife looked back from behind him, and she became a pillar of salt.

Mary Magdalene Was Tormented With Seven Demons

Better news cannot be brought to disciples in tears, than to tell them of Christ's resurrection. And we should study to comfort disciples that are mourners, by telling them whatever we have seen of Christ. It was a wise providence that the proofs of Christ's resurrection were given gradually, and admitted cautiously, that the assurance with which the apostles preached this doctrine afterwards might the more satisfy. Yet how slowly do we admit the consolations which the word of God holds forth! Therefore while Christ comforts his people, he often sees it needful to rebuke and correct them for hardness of heart in distrusting his promise, as well as in not obeying his holy precepts.

Mark 16:9

Now when *Jesus* was risen early the first *day* of the week, he appeared first to Mary Magdalene, out of whom he had cast seven devils.

Mephibosheth Was Crippled

Ishbosheth murdered. David puts to death the murderers. See how Ishbosheth was murdered! When those difficulties dispirit us, which should sharpen our endeavors, we betray both our heavenly crowns and our earthly lives. Love not sleep, lest thou come to poverty and ruin. The idle soul is an easy prey to the destroyer. We know not when and where death will meet us. When we lie down to sleep, we are not sure that we may not sleep the sleep of death before we awake; nor do we know from what hand the death-blow may come.

2 Samuel 4:4

And Jonathan, Saul's son, had a son *that was* lame of *his* feet. He was five years old when the tidings came of Saul and Jonathan out of Jezreel, and his nurse took him up, and fled: and it came to pass, as she made haste to flee, that he fell, and became lame. And his name *was* Mephibosheth

MIRIAM HAD LEPROSY

The cloud departed, and Miriam became leprous. When God goes, evil comes: expect no good when God departs. Aaron, as priest, was judge of the leprosy. He could not pronounce her leprous without trembling, knowing himself to be equally guilty. But if she was thus punished for speaking against Moses, what will become of those who sin against Christ? Aaron, who joined his sister in speaking against Moses, is forced for himself and his sister, to beseech him, and to speak highly of him whom he had so lately blamed. Those who trample upon the saints and servants of God, will one day be glad to make court to them. It is well when rebukes produce confession of sin and repentance. Such offenders, though corrected and disgraced, shall be pardoned. Moses made it appear, that he forgave the injury done him. To this pattern of Moses, and that of our Saviour, who said, "Father, forgive them," we must conform. A reason is given for Miriam's being put out of the camp for seven days; because thus she ought to accept the punishment of her sin. When under the tokens of God's displeasure for sin, it becomes us to take shame to ourselves. This hindered the people's progress in their march forward towards Canaan. Many things oppose us, but nothing so hinders us in the way to heaven, as sin.

Numbers 12:1-10

1 And Miriam and Aaron spake against Moses because of the Ethiopian woman whom he had married: for he had married an Ethiopian woman.

2 And they said, Hath the LORD indeed spoken only by Moses? hath he not spoken also by us? And the LORD heard *it*.

3 (Now the man Moses *was* very meek, above all the men which *were* upon the face of the earth.)

4 And the LORD spake suddenly unto Moses, and unto Aaron, and unto Miriam, Come out ye three unto the tabernacle of the congregation. And they three came out.

5 And the LORD came down in the pillar of the cloud, and stood *in* the door of the tabernacle, and called Aaron and Miriam: and they both came forth.

6 And he said, Hear now my words: If there be a prophet among you, *I* the LORD will make myself known unto him in a vision, *and* will speak unto him in a dream.

7 My servant Moses *is* not so, who *is* faithful in all mine house.

8 With him will I speak mouth to mouth, even apparently, and not in dark speeches; and the similitude of the LORD shall he behold: wherefore then were ye not afraid to speak against my servant Moses?

9 And the anger of the LORD was kindled against them; and he departed.

10 And the cloud departed from off the tabernacle; and, behold, Miriam *became* leprous, *white* as snow: and Aaron looked upon Miriam, and, behold, *she was* leprous

Moses Stuttered

Moses continued backward to the work God designed him for; there was much of cowardice, slothfulness, and unbelief in him. We must not judge of men by the readiness of their discourse. A great deal of wisdom and true worth may be with a slow tongue. God sometimes makes choice of those as his messengers, who have the least of the advantages of art or nature, that his grace in them may appear the more glorious. Christ's disciples were no orators, till the Holy Spirit made them such. God condescends to answer the excuse of Moses. Even self-diffidence, when it hinders us from duty, or clogs us in duty, is very displeasing to the Lord. But while we blame Moses for shrinking from this dangerous service, let us ask our own hearts if we are not neglecting duties easier, and less perilous. The tongue of Aaron, with the head and heart of Moses, would make one completely fit for this errand. God promises, I will be with thy mouth, and with his mouth. Even Aaron, who could speak well, yet could not speak to purpose, unless God gave constant teaching and help; for without the constant aid of Divine grace, the best gifts will fail.

Exodus 4:10-12

10 And Moses said unto the LORD, O my Lord, I *am* not eloquent, neither heretofore, nor since thou hast spoken unto thy servant: but I *am* slow of speech, and of a slow tongue.

11 And the LORD said unto him, Who hath made man's mouth? or who maketh the dumb, or deaf, or the seeing, or the blind? have not I the LORD?

12 Now therefore go, and I will be with thy mouth, and teach thee what thou shalt say.

Noah Got Drunk And His Sons Saw Him Naked

Noah, who had kept sober in drunken company, is now drunk in sober company. Let him that thinks he stands, take heed lest he fall. We have need to be very careful when we use God's good creatures plentifully, lest we use them to excess. The consequence of Noah's sin was shame. Observe here the great evil of the sin of drunkenness. It discovers men; what infirmities they have, they betray when they are drunk; and secrets are then easily got out of them. Drunken porters keep open gates. It disgraces men, and exposes them to contempt. As it shows them, so it shames them. Men say and do that when drunken, which, when sober, they would blush to think of. Notice the care of Shem and Japheth to cover their father's shame. There is a mantle of love to be thrown over the faults of all. Besides that, there is a robe of reverence to be thrown over the faults of parents and other superiors. The blessing of God attends on those who honour their parents, and his curse lights especially on those who dishonor them.

Genesis 9:21-24

21 And he drank of the wine, and was drunken; and he was uncovered within his tent.

22 And Ham, the father of Canaan, saw the nakedness of his father, and told his two brethren without.

23 And Shem and Japheth took a garment, and laid *it* upon both their shoulders, and went backward, and covered the nakedness of their father; and their faces *were* backward, and they saw not their father's nakedness.

24 And Noah awoke from his wine, and knew what his younger son had done unto him.

Other Prophets Were Sawed In Two

It is the excellence of the grace of faith, that, while it helps men to do great things, like Gideon, it keeps from high and great thoughts of themselves. Faith, like Barak's, has recourse unto God in all dangers and difficulties, and then makes grateful returns to God for all mercies and deliverances. By faith, the servants of God shall overcome even the roaring lion that goes about seeking whom he may devour. The believer's faith endures to the end, and, in dying, gives him victory over death and all his deadly enemies, like Samson. The grace of God often fixes upon very undeserving and ill-deserving persons, to do great things for them and by them. But the grace of faith, wherever it is, will put men upon acknowledging God in all their ways, as Jephthah. It will make men bold and courageous in a good cause. Few ever met with greater trials, few ever showed more lively faith, than David, and he has left a testimony as to the trials and acts of faith, in the book of Psalms, which has been, and ever will be, of great value to the people of God. Those are likely to grow up to be distinguished for faith, who begin betimes, like Samuel, to exercise it. And faith will enable a man to serve God and his generation, in whatever way he may be employed. The interests and powers of kings and kingdoms are often opposed to God and his people; but God can easily subdue all that set themselves against him. It is a greater honour and happiness to work righteousness than to work miracles. By faith we have comfort of the promises; and by faith we are prepared to wait for the promises, and in due time to receive them. And though we do not hope to have our dead relatives or friends restored to life in this world, yet faith will support under the loss of them, and direct to the hope of a better resurrection. Shall we be most amazed at the wickedness of human nature, that it is capable of such awful cruelties to fellow-creatures, or at the excellence of Divine grace, that is able to bear up the faithful under such cruelties, and to carry them safely through all? What a difference between God's judgement of a saint, and man's judgment! The world is not worthy of those scorned, persecuted saints, whom their persecutors reckon unworthy to live. They are not worthy of their company, example, counsel, or other benefits. For they know not what a saint is, nor the worth of a saint, nor how to use him; they hate, and drive such away, as they do the offer of Christ and his grace.

Hebrews 11: 37-40

37 They were stoned, they were sawn asunder, were tempted, were slain
with the sword: they wandered about in sheepskins and goatskins; being
destitute, afflicted, tormented;
38 (Of whom the world was not worthy:) they wandered in deserts,
and *in* mountains, and *in* dens and caves of the earth.
39 And these all, having obtained a good report through faith, received
not the promise:
40 God having provided some better thing for us, that they without
us should not be made perfect.

Paul Had A Thorn In His Flesh

The apostle gives an account of the method God took to keep him humble, and to prevent his being lifted up above measure, on account of the visions and revelations he had. We are not told what this thorn in the flesh was, whether some great trouble, or some great temptation. But God often brings this good out of evil, that the reproaches of our enemies help to hide pride from us. If God loves us, he will keep us from being exalted above measure; and spiritual burdens are ordered to cure spiritual pride. This thorn in the flesh is said to be a messenger of Satan which he sent for evil; but God designed it, and overruled it for good. Prayer is a salve for every sore, a remedy for every malady; and when we are afflicted with thorns in the flesh, we should give ourselves to prayer. If an answer be not given to the first prayer, nor to the second, we are to continue praying. Troubles are sent to teach us to pray; and are continued, to teach us to continue instant in prayer. Though God accepts the prayer of faith, yet he does not always give what is asked for: as he sometimes grants in wrath, so he sometimes denies in love. When God does not take away our troubles and temptations, yet, if he gives grace enough for us, we have no reason to complain. Grace signifies the good-will of God towards us, and that is enough to enlighten and enliven us, sufficient to strengthen and comfort in all afflictions and distresses. His strength is made perfect in our weakness. Thus, his grace is manifested and magnified. When we are weak in ourselves, then we are strong in the grace of our Lord Jesus Christ; when we feel that we are weak in ourselves, then we go to Christ, receive strength from him, and enjoy most the supplies of Divine strength and grace. We owe it to good men, to stand up in the defense of their reputation; and we are under special obligations to those from whom we have received benefit, especially spiritual benefit, to own them as instruments in God's hand of good to us. Here is an account of the apostle's behavior and kind intentions; in which see the character of a faithful minister of the gospel. This was his great aim and design, to do good. Here are noticed several sins commonly found among professors of religion. Falls and misdeeds are humbling to a minister; and God sometimes takes this way to humble those who might be tempted to be lifted up. These vast verses show to what excesses the false teachers had drawn aside their deluded followers. How grievous it is that such evils should be found among professors of the gospel! Yet thus it is, and has been too often, and it was so even in the days of the apostles.

2 Corinthians 12:7-10

7 And lest I should be exalted above measure through the abundance of the revelations, there was given to me a thorn in the flesh, the messenger of Satan to buffet me, lest I should be exalted above measure.

8 For this thing I besought the Lord thrice, that it might depart from me.

9 And he said unto me, My grace is sufficient for thee: for my strength is made perfect in weakness. Most gladly therefore will I rather glory in my infirmities, that the power of Christ may rest upon me.

10 Therefore I take pleasure in infirmities, in reproaches, in necessities, in persecutions, in distresses for Christ's sake: for when I am weak, then am I strong.

Peter Frequently Put His Foot In His Mouth

Peter felt sure that his Master was ready to do what was right. Christ spoke first to give him proof that no thought can be withheld from him. We must never decline our duty for fear of giving offence; but we must sometimes deny ourselves in our worldly interests, rather than give offence. However, the money was lodged in the fish, He who knows all things alone could know it, and only almighty power could bring it to Peter's hook. The power and the poverty of Christ should be mentioned together. If called by providence to be poor, like our Lord, let us trust in his power, and our God shall supply all our need, according to his riches in glory by Christ Jesus. In the way of obedience, in the course, perhaps, of our usual calling, as he helped Peter, so he will help us. And if any sudden call should occur, which we are not prepared to meet, let us not apply to others, till we first seek Christ.

Matthew 17:24-27;

24 And when they were come to Capernaum, they that received tribute *money* came to Peter, and said, Doth not your master pay tribute?

25 He saith, Yes. And when he was come into the house, Jesus prevented him, saying, What thinkest thou, Simon? of whom do the kings of the earth take custom or tribute? of their own children, or of strangers?

26 Peter saith unto him, Of strangers. Jesus saith unto him, Then are the children free.

27 Notwithstanding, lest we should offend them, go thou to the sea, and cast an hook, and take up the fish that first cometh up; and when thou hast opened his mouth, thou shalt find a piece of money: that take, and give unto them for me and thee.

Peter Was Crucified Upside Down On A Cross

Stretch forth thy hands refers to crucifixion, where a person's hands and arms are stretched out and nailed to the crossbeam. Tradition says Peter chose to be crucified upside down because he felt himself unworthy of dying in the same exact manner as Jesus. Our Lord addressed Peter by his original name, as if he had forfeited that of Peter through his denying him. He now answered, Thou knowest that I love thee; but without professing to love Jesus more than others. We must not be surprised to have our sincerity called into question, when we ourselves have done that which makes it doubtful. Every remembrance of past sins, even pardoned sins, renews the sorrow of a true penitent. Conscious of integrity, Peter solemnly appealed to Christ, as knowing all things, even the secrets of his heart. It is well when our falls and mistakes make us more humble and watchful. The sincerity of our love to God must be brought to the test; and it behooves us to inquire with earnest, preserving prayer to the heart-searching God, to examine and prove us, whether we are able to stand this test. No one can be qualified to feed the sheep and lambs of Christ, who does not love the good Shepherd more than any earthly advantage or object. It is the great concern of every good man, whatever death he dies, to glorify God in it; for what is our chief end but this, to die to the Lord, at the word of the Lord?

John 21:18-19

18 Verily, verily, I say unto thee, When thou wast young, thou girdedst thyself, and walkedst whither thou wouldest: but when thou shalt be old, thou shalt stretch forth thy hands, and another shall gird thee, and carry *thee* whither thou wouldest not.

19 This spake he, signifying by what death he should glorify God. And when he had spoken this, he saith unto him, Follow me.

Peter's Mother-In-Law Had A High Fever

Peter had a wife, yet was an apostle of Christ, who showed that he approved of the married state, by being thus kind to Peter's wife's relations. The church of Rome, which forbids ministers to marry, goes contrary to that apostle upon whom they rest so much. He had his wife's mother with him in his family, which is an example to be kind to our relations. In spiritual healing, the Scripture speaks the word, the Spirit gives the touch, touches the heart, touches the hand. Those who recover from fevers, commonly are weak and feeble sometime after; but to show that this cure was above the power of nature, the woman was at once so well as to go about the business of the house. The miracles which Jesus did being noised abroad, many thronged to him. He healed all that were sick, though the patient was ever so mean, and the case ever so bad. Many are the diseases and calamities to which we are liable in the body; and there is more, in those words of the gospel, that Jesus Christ bore our sicknesses and carried our sorrows, to support and comfort us under them, than in all the writings of the philosophers. Let us not grudge labor, trouble, or expense in doing good to others.

Matthew 8:14-15

14And when Jesus was come into Peter's house, he saw his wife's mother laid, and sick of a fever.

15 And he touched her hand, and the fever left her: and she arose, and ministered unto them.

Rachel Lied To Her Father, Was Cursed And Died In Childbirth

God can put a bridle in the mouth of wicked men, to restrain their malice, though he does not change their hearts. Though they have no love to God's people, they will pretend to it, and try to make a merit of necessity. Foolish Laban! to call those things his gods which could be stolen! Enemies may steal our goods, but not our God. Here Laban lays to Jacob's charge things that he knew not. Those who commit their cause to God, are not forbidden to plead it themselves with meekness and fear. When we read of Rachel's stealing her father's images, what a scene of iniquity opens! The family of Nahor, who left the idolatrous Chaldees; is this family itself become idolatrous? It is even so. The truth seems to be, that they were like some in after-times, who swore by the Lord and by Malcham, and like others in our times, who wish to serve both God and mammon. Great numbers will acknowledge the true God in words, but their hearts and houses are the abodes of spiritual idolatry. When a man gives himself up to covetousness, like Laban, the world is his god; and he has only to reside among gross idolaters in order to become one, or at least a favorer of their abominations.

Genesis 31:35

35 And she said to her father, Let it not displease my lord that I cannot rise up before thee; for the custom of women *is* upon me. And he searched, but found not the images.

Rachel had passionately said, Give me children, or else I die; and now that she had children, she died! The death of the body is but the departure of the soul to the world of spirits. When shall we learn that it is God alone who really knows what is best for his people, and that in all worldly affairs the safest path for the Christian is to say from the heart, It is the Lord, let him do what seemeth him good. Here alone is our safety and our comfort, to know no will but his. Her dying lips called her newborn son Ben-oni, the son of my sorrow; and many a son proves to be the heaviness of her that bare him. Children are enough the sorrow of their mothers; they should, therefore, when they grow up, study to be their joy, and so, if possible, to make them some amends. But Jacob, because he would not renew the sorrowful remembrance of the mother's death every time he called his son, changed his name to Benjamin, the son of my right hand: that is, very dear to me; the support of my age, like the staff in my right hand'

Genesis 35:13-20 RACHEL IS CURSED AND DIES

13 And God went up from him in the place where he talked with him.

14 And Jacob set up a pillar in the place where he talked with him, *even* a pillar of stone: and he poured a drink offering thereon, and he poured oil thereon.

15 And Jacob called the name of the place where God spake with him, Bethel.

16 And they journeyed from Bethel; and there was but a little way to come to Ephrath: and Rachel travailed, and she had hard labour.

17 And it came to pass, when she was in hard labour, that the midwife said unto her, Fear not; thou shalt have this son also.

18 And it came to pass, as her soul was in departing, (for she died) that she called his name Benoni: but his father called him Benjamin.

19 And Rachel died, and was buried in the way to Ephrath, which *is* Bethlehem.

20 And Jacob set a pillar upon her grave: that *is* the pillar of Rachel's grave unto this day.

Sarai, Hannah, Rachel And Elizabeth Were Barren

Children are the chief of these blessings. Heritage - Only from God's blessing, even as an inheritance is not the fruit of a man's own labour, but the gift of God. Shall I, I, that in the ordinary course of my providence use to give a birth to women, to whom I have given a power to conceive, shall I not give a birth to my people, whom by my promises I have made to conceive such expectations? And shut - Nor shall Zion once only bring forth, but she shall go on, her womb shall not be shut, she shall every day bring forth more and more children, and my presence shall be with my church, to the end of the world.

Genesis 11:29-31-Sarai was barren
1 Samuel 1:1-5-Hannah was barren
Genesis 29:30-31- Rachel is barren
Luke 1:7-Elizabeth was barren
Genesis 11:29-30

29 And Abram and Nahor took them wives: the name of Abram's wife *was* Sarai; and the name of Nahor's wife, Milcah, the daughter of Haran, the father of Milcah, and the father of Iscah.
30 But Sarai was barren; she *had* no child

1 Samuel 1 1:5

But unto Hannah he gave a worthy portion; for he loved Hannah: but the LORD had shut up her womb.

Genesis 29: 31

31 And when the LORD saw that Leah *was* hated, he opened her womb: but Rachel *was* barren.

Luke 1: 5-7

5 There was in the days of Herod, the king of Judaea, a certain priest named Zacharias, of the course of Abia: and his wife *was* of the daughters of Aaron, and her name *was* Elisabeth.

6 And they were both righteous before God, walking in all the commandments and ordinances of the Lord blameless.

7 And they had no child, because that Elisabeth was barren, and they both were *now* well stricken in years.

Saul Was Jealous Over David

David's troubles not only immediately follow his triumphs, but arise from them; such is the vanity of that which seems greatest in this world. It is a sign that the Spirit of God is departed from men, if, like Saul, they are peevish, envious, suspicious, and ill-natured. Compare David, with his harp in his hand, aiming to serve Saul, and Saul, with his javelin in his hand, aiming to slay David; and observe the sweetness and usefulness of God's persecuted people, and the barbarity of their persecutors. But David's safety must be ascribed to God's providence. For a long time David was kept in continual apprehension of falling by the hand of Saul, yet he persevered in meek and respectful behavior towards his persecutor. How uncommon is such prudence and discretion, especially under insults and provocations! Let us inquire if we imitate this part of the exemplary character before us. Are we behaving wisely in all our ways? Is there no sinful omission, no rashness of spirit, nothing wrong in our conduct? Opposition and perverseness in others, will not excuse wrong tempers in us, but should increase our care, and attention to the duties of our station. Consider Him that endured contradiction of sinners against himself, lest ye be weary and faint in your minds, If David magnified the honour of being son-in-law to king Saul, how should we magnify the honour of being sons to the King of kings!

1 Samuel 18:7-12.

7 And the women answered *one another* as they played, and said, Saul hath slain his thousands, and David his ten thousands.

8 And Saul was very wroth, and the saying displeased him; and he said, They have ascribed unto David ten thousands, and to me they have ascribed *but* thousands: and *what* can he have more but the kingdom?

9 And Saul eyed David from that day and forward.

10 And it came to pass on the morrow, that the evil spirit from God came upon Saul, and he prophesied in the midst of the house: and David played with his hand, as at other times: and *there was* a javelin in Saul's hand.

11 And Saul cast the javelin; for he said, I will smite David even to the wall *with it*. And David avoided out of his presence twice.

12 And Saul was afraid of David, because the LORD was with him, and was departed from Saul.

Saul, His Sons, And His Servant Died On The Same Day

The Scripture makes no mention what became of the souls of Saul and his sons, after they were dead; but of their bodies only: secret things belong not to us. It is of little consequence by what means we die, or what is done with our dead bodies. If our souls are saved, our bodies will be raised incorruptible and glorious; but not to fear His wrath, who is able to destroy both body and soul in hell, is the extreme of folly and wickedness. How useless is the respect of fellow-creatures to those who are suffering the wrath of God! While pompous funerals, grand monuments, and he praises of men, honour the memory of the deceased, the soul may be suffering in the regions of darkness and despair! Let us seek that honour which cometh from God only.

1 Samuel 31:2-6

2 And the Philistines followed hard upon Saul and upon his sons; and the Philistines slew Jonathan, and Abinadab, and Malchishua, Saul's sons.

3 And the battle went sore against Saul, and the archers hit him; and he was sore wounded of the archers.

4 Then said Saul unto his armourbearer, Draw thy sword, and thrust me through therewith; lest these uncircumcised come and thrust me through, and abuse me. But his armourbearer would not; for he was sore afraid. Therefore Saul took a sword, and fell upon it.

5 And when his armourbearer saw that Saul was dead, he fell likewise upon his sword, and died with him.

6 So Saul died, and his three sons, and his armourbearer, and all his men, that same day together.

Solomon Was Married To 700 Women And Had 300 Concubines

There is not a more melancholy and astonishing instance of human depravity in the sacred Scriptures, than that here recorded. Solomon became a public worshipper of abominable idols! Probably he by degrees gave way to pride and luxury, and thus lost his relish for true wisdom. Nothing forms in itself a security against the deceitfulness and depravity of the human heart. Nor will old age cure the heart of any evil propensity. If our sinful passions are not crucified and mortified by the grace of God, they never will die of themselves, but will last even when opportunities to gratify them are taken away. Let him that thinks he stands, take heed lest he fall. We see how weak we are of ourselves, without the grace of God; let us therefore live in constant dependence on that grace. Let us watch and be sober: ours is a dangerous warfare, and in an enemy's country, while our worst foes are the traitors in our own hearts.

1 Kings 11:1-4

1 But king Solomon loved many strange women, together with the daughter of Pharaoh, women of the Moabites, Ammonites, Edomites, Zidonians, *and* Hittites;

2 Of the nations *concerning* which the LORD said unto the children of Israel, Ye shall not go in to them, neither shall they come in unto you: *for* surely they will turn away your heart after their gods: Solomon clave unto these in love.

3 And he had seven hundred wives, princesses, and three hundred concubines: and his wives turned away his heart.

4 For it came to pass, when Solomon was old, *that* his wives turned away his heart after other gods: and his heart was not perfect with the LORD his God, as *was* the heart of David his father.

Stephen Was Stoned

Nothing is so comfortable to dying saints, or so encouraging to suffering saints, as to see Jesus at the right hand of God: blessed be God, by faith we may see him there. Our Lord Jesus is God, to whom we are to seek, and in whom we are to trust and comfort ourselves, living and dying. Here is a prayer for his persecutors. Though the sin was very great, yet if they would lay it to their hearts, God would not lay it to their charge. Stephen died as much in a hurry as ever any man did, yet, when he died, the words used are, he fell asleep; he applied himself to his dying work with as much composure as if he had been going to sleep. He shall awake again in the morning of the resurrection, to be received into the presence of the Lord, where is fulness of joy, and to share the pleasures that are at his right hand, for evermore.

Acts 7:55-60

55 But he, being full of the Holy Ghost, looked up stedfastly into heaven, and saw the glory of God, and Jesus standing on the right hand of God,

56 And said, Behold, I see the heavens opened, and the Son of man standing on the right hand of God.

57 Then they cried out with a loud voice, and stopped their ears, and ran upon him with one accord,

58 And cast *him* out of the city, and stoned *him*: and the witnesses laid down their clothes at a young man's feet, whose name was Saul.

59 And they stoned Stephen, calling upon *God*, and saying, Lord Jesus, receive my spirit.

60 And he kneeled down, and cried with a loud voice, Lord, lay not this sin to their charge. And when he had said this, he fell asleep.

Tamar Was Raped By Her Brother; Then That Brother Was Killed By Another Brother

From henceforward David was followed with one trouble after another. Adultery and murder were David's sins, the like sins among his children were the beginnings of his punishment: he was too indulgent to his children. Thus David might trace the sins of his children to his own misconduct, which must have made the anguish of the chastisement worse. Let no one ever expect good treatment from those who are capable of attempting their seduction; but it is better to suffer the greatest wrong than to commit the least sin. Observe the aggravations of Absalom's sin: he would have Ammon slain, when least fit to go out of the world. He engaged his servants in the guilt. Those servants are ill-taught who obey wicked masters, against God's commands. Indulged children always prove crosses to godly parents, whose foolish love leads them to neglect their duty to God. Jonadab was as guilty of Ammon's death, as of his sin; such false friends do they prove, who counsel us to do wickedly. Instead of loathing Absalom as a murderer, David, after a time, longed to go forth to him. This was David's infirmity: God saw something in his heart that made a difference, else we should have thought that he, as much as Eli, honored his sons more than God.

2 Samuel 13:1-14

10 And Amnon said unto Tamar, Bring the meat into the chamber, that I may eat of thine hand. And Tamar took the cakes which she had made, and brought *them* into the chamber to Amnon her brother.

11 And when she had brought *them* unto him to eat, he took hold of her, and said unto her, Come lie with me, my sister.

12 And she answered him, Nay, my brother, do not force me; for no such thing ought to be done in Israel: do not thou this folly.

13 And I, whither shall I cause my shame to go? and as for thee, thou shalt be as one of the fools in Israel. Now therefore, I pray thee, speak unto the king; for he will not withhold me from thee.

14 Howbeit he would not hearken unto her voice: but, being stronger than she, forced her, and lay with her.

2 Samuel 13:22, 27-28

22 And Absalom spake unto his brother Amnon neither good nor bad: for Absalom hated Amnon, because he had forced his sister Tamar.

27 But Absalom pressed him, that he let Amnon and all the king's sons go with him.

28 Now Absalom had commanded his servants, saying, Mark ye now when Amnon's heart is merry with wine, and when I say unto you, Smite Amnon; then kill him, fear not: have not I commanded you? be courageous, and be valiant.

The Earth Swallowed Up The Sons Of Korah

Moses did not number the people but when God commanded him. We have here the families registered, as well as the tribes. The total was nearly the same as when numbered at mount Sinai. Notice is here taken of the children of Korah; they died not, as the children of Dathan and Abiram; they seem not to have joined even their own father in rebellion. If we partake not of the sins of sinners, we shall not partake of their plagues.

Numbers 26:1-4, 10-11

1 And it came to pass after the plague, that the LORD spake unto
Moses and unto Eleazar the son of Aaron the priest, saying,
2 Take the sum of all the congregation of the children of Israel, from
twenty years old and upward, throughout their fathers' house, all that are
able to go to war in Israel.
3 And Moses and Eleazar the priest spake with them in the plains of
Moab by Jordan *near* Jericho, saying,
4 *Take the sum of the people*, from twenty years old and upward; as the
LORD commanded Moses and the children of Israel, which went forth
out of the land of Egypt.
10 And the earth opened her mouth, and swallowed them up together
with Korah, when that company died, what time the fire devoured two
hundred and fifty men: and they became a sign.
11 Notwithstanding the children of Korah died not.

Thomas Doubted

This was the first day of the week, and this day is afterwards often mentioned by the sacred writers; for it was evidently set apart as the Christian sabbath, in remembrance of Christ's resurrection. The disciples had shut the doors for fear of the Jews; and when they had no such expectation, Jesus himself came and stood in the midst of them, having miraculously, though silently, opened the doors. It is a comfort to Christ's disciples, when their assemblies can only be held in private, that no doors can shut out Christ's presence. When He manifests his love to believers by the comforts of his Spirit, he assures them that because he lives, they shall live also. A sight of Christ will gladden the heart of a disciple at any time; and the more we see of Jesus, the more we shall rejoice. He said, Receive ye the Holy Ghost, thus showing that their spiritual life, as well as all their ability for their work, would be derived from him, and depended upon him. Every word of Christ which is received in the heart by faith, comes accompanied by this Divine breathing; and without this there is neither light nor life. Nothing is seen, known, discerned, or felt of God, but through this. After this, Christ directed the apostles to declare the only method by which sin would be forgiven. This power did not exist at all in the apostles as a power to give judgment, but only as a power to declare the character of those whom God would accept or reject in the day of judgment. They have clearly laid down the marks whereby a child of God may be discerned and be distinguished from a false professor; and according to what they have declared shall every case be decided in the day of judgment. When we assemble in Christ's name, especially on his holy day, he will meet with us, and speak peace to us. The disciples of Christ should endeavor to build up one another in their most holy faith, both by repeating what they have heard to those that were absent, and by making known what they have experienced. Thomas limited the Holy One of Israel, when he would be convinced by his own method or not at all. He might justly have been left in his unbelief, after rejecting such abundant proofs. The fears and sorrows of the disciples are often lengthened, to punish their negligence. That one day in seven should be religiously observed, was an appointment from the beginning. And that, in the kingdom of the Messiah, the first day of the week should be that solemn day, was pointed out, in that Christ on that day once and again met his disciples in a religious assembly. The religious observance of that day has come down to us through every age of the church. There is not an unbelieving word in our tongues, nor thought in our minds, but it is known to the Lord Jesus; and he was pleased to accommodate himself even to Thomas, rather than leave him in his unbelief. We ought thus to bear with the weak. This warning is given to all. If we are faithless, we are Christless and graceless, hopeless and joyless. Thomas was ashamed of his unbelief, and cried out, My Lord and my God. He spoke with affection, as one that took hold of Christ with all his might; "My Lord and my God." Sound and sincere believers, though slow and weak, shall be graciously accepted of the Lord Jesus. It is the duty of those who read and hear the gospel, to believe, to embrace the doctrine of Christ, and that record concerning him.

John 20:24-29

24 But Thomas, one of the twelve, called Didymus, was not with them when Jesus came.

25 The other disciples therefore said unto him, We have seen the Lord. But he said unto them, Except I shall see in his hands the print of the nails, and put my finger into the print of the nails, and thrust my hand into his side, I will not believe.

26 And after eight days again his disciples were within, and Thomas with them: *then* came Jesus, the doors being shut, and stood in the midst, and said, Peace *be* unto you.

27 Then saith he to Thomas, Reach hither thy finger, and behold my hands; and reach hither thy hand, and thrust *it* into my side: and be not faithless, but believing.

28 And Thomas answered and said unto him, My Lord and my God.

29 Jesus saith unto him, Thomas, because thou hast seen me, thou hast believed: blessed *are* they that have not seen, and *yet* have believed.

Zedekiah And Samson's Eyes Were Gouged Out

At length the city was taken by storm. The king, his family, and his great men escaped in the night, by secret passages. But those deceive themselves who think to escape God's judgments, as much as those who think to brave them. By what befell Zedekiah, two prophecies, which seemed to contradict each other, were both fulfilled. Jeremiah prophesied that Zedekiah should be brought to Babylon, that he should not see Babylon. He was brought thither, but his eyes being put out, he did not see it.

2 Kings 25:5-7

5 And the army of the Chaldees pursued after the king, and overtook him in the plains of Jericho: and all his army were scattered from him.

6 So they took the king, and brought him up to the king of Babylon to Riblah; and they gave judgment upon him.

7 And they slew the sons of Zedekiah before his eyes, and put out the eyes of Zedekiah, and bound him with fetters of brass, and carried him to Babylon.

Judges 16:20-22

20 And she said, The Philistines *be* upon thee, Samson. And he awoke out of his sleep, and said, I will go out as at other times before, and shake myself. And he wist not that the LORD was departed from him.

21 But the Philistines took him, and put out his eyes, and brought him down to Gaza, and bound him with fetters of brass; and he did grind in the prison house.

22 Howbeit the hair of his head began to grow again after he was shaven.

CPSIA information can be obtained
at www.ICGtesting.com
Printed in the USA
BVHW071354130519
548119BV00007B/697/P

9 781546 279525